Librarians & Stereotypes:
So, Now What?

By
Christina J. Steffy, M.L.I.S.

Peer reviewers
Christine Iannicelli, M.L.I.S.
Heather Simoneau, M.L.I.S.
Claire Van Ens, Ph.D.

Librarians & Stereotypes: So, Now What?

Copyright © 2015 by Christina J. Steffy

Cover created by Christina J. Steffy using Tagul (htttps://tagul.com)

Author information
LinkedIn: www.linkedin.com/in/cjsteffy
Twitter: @LIS_QueenB
Email: cjsteffy@gmail.com

Printed in the United States of America
ISBN: 978-0-9852599-6-9

Published by

Crave Press

www.cravepress.com

TABLE OF CONTENTS

Preface	1
Chapter 1: Why Should We Bother Studying Stereotypes?	5
Chapter 2: Librarianship's Historical Influence on Stereotypes	13
Chapter 3: Librarian Stereotypes	19
Chapter 4: Culture and Theories Impacting Stereotype Development	33
Chapter 5: The Sexy Librarian Stereotype and Its Impact on the Profession	69
Chapter 6: Public Perceptions of Librarians and Libraries	79
Chapter 7: Librarians and Stereotypes Survey	93
Chapter 8: So, Now What?	121
References and Bibliography	141
Appendix	155
About the Author	159

PREFACE

I did not originally intend to write this book; instead, I initially set out to make a poster display in my library that showed some famous librarians in pop culture. These were, of course, more recent or very popular representations that my students would recognize and think added a sense of "coolness" to the profession. I wanted to do that not only because I've always been a big proponent of dispelling stereotypes but also because I wanted to show that research can be fun (or at least interesting). There are even some fields where research can save the world, maybe not to the scale of how Giles's research helped save the world in *Buffy the Vampire Slayer*, but in some fields, particularly in my students' nursing field, research is necessary to save lives. I also wanted people to see that not all research is done in books anymore, nor is it all done online — your resources depend on what you need to find out. Once I started looking at pop culture figures to include on the poster, I began thinking of parlaying this into an article; however, upon mentioning this to my husband, he suggested I write a book about the subject. That hadn't crossed my mind at first because of the scope of the project, but I decided I was too excited about this topic to not take on the challenge. Thus I began my research to learn more about librarian stereotypes.

In addition to having an academic interest in stereotypes, I've also found myself dealing with stereotypes personally to the point where I'm exhausted from hearing them. Finally, my background in English and communication has exposed me to various interdisciplinary social theories, and I often find myself thinking about these theories as I read or observe interactions. I couldn't help but start looking at librarian stereotypes through the lens of these theories, and I also couldn't help but notice the small amount of literature available that examines library stereotypes through theories outside of the field of librarianship.

Although the idea to incorporate theories from outside of the profession came up fairly early in the process, it took some time to determine my focus and the structure of the book. My initial intent was to look at various librarian representations in pop culture in chronological order to show the progression of the stereotypes and then look at how we are presenting ourselves now and how that self-representation is shaping the views of the profession. After some preliminary research, though, I nixed that idea. The profession doesn't need another article or book looking at representations of librarians and applying stereotypes to them. I did notice what was missing was a thorough examination of the ways concepts from fields outside of library science — in the case of this book, the fields of communications, literature, gender studies, cultural studies, psychology, sociology, and anthropology — influenced the creation and perpetuation of stereotypes and the level of professionalism society affords the field. Pagowsky and DeFrain (2014) and Pagowsky and Rigby (2014) even admit this need to look at the profession from the points of view of other fields, and Pagowsky and Rigby recently published a book on the topic. I noticed what was also missing was the "why" behind why librarians represent themselves the way they do rather than just an observation of the representations that are out there. This "why" is important because it helps us understand how stereotypes are impacting the way we think about ourselves in the profession. There was also a bigger question lurking in the background of the published literature that was never brought to the surface: Will our society's culture ever allow the profession to truly be seen as "professional," or will it always be seen as a "semi-professional" women's field?

This book is my attempt to bring all of my knowledge, experience, and inquisitiveness together to address these issues and questions and hopefully to open the door to examining library and information science through the lenses of other fields.

CHAPTER 1

Why Should We Bother Studying Stereotypes?

"Why did you decide to become a librarian? Was it a love of books?"

"Ooooo, you're a librarian?" (said in a sexually suggestive tone of voice)

"So...what do you actually do?"

"You're a librarian? I guess you need to be good with computers to do that?"

Those quotes are some of the responses the author of this book has received when telling people she's a librarian. The first two responses represent two dominant librarian stereotypes — we only work with books, and the sexy librarian. The third represents a problem that encourages people to fill in their knowledge gaps with stereotypes — confusion about what it is we do. The fourth response represents a more modern idea of librarians, yet it could foreshadow an emerging librarian as IT person stereotype. Clearly librarian stereotypes have become so common that they work their way into daily conversations as default assumptions; thus it is important to study stereotypes despite the fact that an overwhelming amount of literature exists on the topic.

Admittedly, librarians are professionals obsessed with stereotypes. It's no secret that an abundance of literature engaged in extensive "navel gazing" exists in this field. But most of that literature is based solely on ideas from within the profession and is examined solely through the lens of librarianship. Also, most of the literature observes the representations, categorizes them, and discusses what this means for how people see the profession. The literature certainly paints a detailed progression of stereotypes and both fictional and non-fictional figures that embody or refute these stereotypes. Unfortunately the literature by and large observes, analyzes, and philosophizes through the lens of librarianship, leading us to believe that we must either fit stereotypes or defy them; the literature also leads us to believe that we can impact the way the world views the profession. This information about stereotypes and embodiments or refutations of them is important, and it provides a solid base for research to continue to examine other aspects of stereotypes and their implications for the profession; however, the literature doesn't extend beyond this base, and it leaves many questions unanswered. These unanswered questions include:

- Why do librarians represent themselves the way they do? We often see the finished product and we analyze it and make assumptions about its creator, but we need to get to the "Why?" behind the finished product. If the "Why?" is to refute stereotypes, is it working?
- Are stereotypes influencing librarians themselves in positive or negative ways, or are they not influencing librarians at all?
- Can we ever actually shake the stereotypes that are in place, or have our culture, language, and psychology ingrained certain stereotypes in our nature?
- Is the media perpetuating certain stereotypes? If it is, will it be possible to defy these stereotypes? After all, the media paints a grim historic picture of the depictions of librarians.
- As we try to defy some stereotypes, are we creating new stereotypes? And if we are creating new stereotypes, are these new stereotypes helping or hurting the profession?

- Are *we* actually changing stereotypes, or are they changing organically because of cultural attitudes?
- So what? Are stereotypes really that important? The literature does cover this historically, but will they continue to be important in the future?

It is true that these questions may never be answered completely or at all, but they need to be asked. Also, as Pagowsky and DeFrain (2014) state, "We urge, as Still and Wilkinson (2014) have stressed, that librarianship as a profession be studied in greater depth in fields outside of librarianship, such as psychology and sociology" (para. 6). Thus in order to get to the root of the aforementioned questions, this book examines the profession and its stereotypes through the lenses of social science fields other than librarianship.

But should we even care about librarian stereotypes anymore? With the dearth of literature on the topic, even when that literature leaves many questions unanswered, haven't we exhausted this topic? And how big of an impact can stereotypes have anyway? Attebury (2010) refers to Wilson's 1982 writings that question whether or not it's a good idea to continue the stereotype discussion: "Wilson (1982) suggests that repeated reference to stereotypes often serves only to ingrain the stereotypes further into our consciousness. She advocates only talking about stereotypes when something positive can be said about them" (p. 9). However Keer and Carlos (2014) point out that stereotypes that seem positive may still have underlying negative effects and/or assumptions: "In fact, because they seem harmless on the surface, they are more damaging and more difficult to resist" ("Stereotypes," para. 2).

Padavic and Reskin (2002) tell us that "stereotypes are 'overlearned,' which means that they are habitual and automatic. As a result, they influence our perceptions and behaviors without our awareness" (p. 43). When subconscious ideas of something impact our perceptions and awareness of the world around us, especially if those ideas are often incorrect, it is important to bring these ideas to light and correct them. The fact that libraries continue to fight for funding because school administrators continue to think that school librarians aren't needed is an indication that the world has certain ideas about what we do, and these ideas are by and large incorrect; this isn't always due to stereotypes, but the stereotypes that exist about librarianship do not portray an accurate picture of our profession and no doubt contribute to this thinking. An example of the public seeing librarians, particularly school librarians, as "a dying breed" and an outdated profession being replaced by Google occurred in early 2014 in Bloomsburg, Pennsylvania. Bloomsburg Area School District planned to eliminate its high school librarian position once the current librarian retired. The librarian would be replaced by an aide, and the elementary school librarian would cover both schools. It was assumed research and citation skills were being taught by English teachers. "The administration perceived that the librarian essentially ran a 'study hall' and reasoned that an aide could do the same thing at less pay" (Neyer, 2014, p. 109). The high school principal claimed "having a 21st-century librarian was a 'luxury' for the district, not a necessity" (Neyer, 2014, p. 110). After much support from the community, including from school teachers, parents, public librarians, and a Bloomsburg University librarian, the school decided to maintain and fill the position with a full-time librarian rather than replace the position with an aide, but it took people both inside and outside of the profession advocating for the retention of this position. Sadly the thought that the librarian was a glorified study hall monitor existed in a town that also contains a public university. Despite what would be assumed to be a supportive environment that understands the value of a library in education and preparing students for college, this school district administration still saw librarianship as an outdated profession that really didn't do anything to help students achieve academically.

But there are more consequences of stereotypes than funding, and there is more to consider than whether or not the stereotypes can be changed. Stereotypes impact patron interactions with librarians and libraries because stereotypes may lead these patrons to have certain incorrect ideas about what a librarian does, how smart a librarian is, and what resources libraries have available. According to Pho and Masland (2014), "Students may approach the library with certain expectations because this imagery of library fear and anxiety is communicated to them through the media. For example, students may have anxiety about approaching the reference desk for help or expect the library to only have books to aid them in their research…A lack of understanding of library resources can result in visiting the library less frequently" ("Librarian Stereotypes," para. 2). Patrons may already be vulnerable and have anxiety about asking for help related to their research needs; for example a patron may feel ashamed to ask for help searching for jobs, or a college patron who can't find what he is looking for on Google may feel stupid because he thinks Google has everything and he should be able to find what he's looking for quickly and easily. When people already have high levels of anxiety and emotion they don't want to add to it by approaching someone who won't be able to help them, or they are afraid and ashamed to approach someone who may be able to help them because they think this person will be a "know it all" who is mean and doesn't want to interact with people.

So why are we focusing on how people see us, then, instead of what resources are available to people? Shouldn't our resources matter more than whether we look intimidating or old or some other stereotype? West (2011) says, "Our patrons take their cues from us. They see a library and think, 'This is what a library is. This is how a library works.' We have a responsibility to that image. Not to our personal image per se...but [to] the idea of what a library is and how the business of managing information works" (p. 127). This is true — we do have a responsibility to the image of the profession as a whole and to helping people understand what the profession is, what it entails, and what libraries can offer them; however it's naïve to overlook the fact that our personal image is tied into this view of the profession. When we come into contact with someone who works in a profession, the social and visual cues this person provides often symbolize professions for us. "A person in a white coat isn't a scientist and someone in a tweed jacket isn't a professor. These are representations of professions and the people who practice them. People are different from their professions, although they may strongly identify with them. Many jobs are defined in our collective mind by symbols like these" (Tobias, 2003, p. 13). These symbols carry stereotypical ideas with them that are hard to shake; however, first impressions of people also lead to ideas that are hard to shake. These impressions are often gleaned when a patron first looks at a librarian, and they influence whether or not a patron will even approach a librarian. "As minimal an exposure time as a tenth of a second is sufficient for people to make a specific trait inference from facial appearance. Additional exposure time increases confidence in judgments and allows for more differentiated trait impressions. However, the judgments are already anchored on the initial inference" (Willis and Todorov, 2008, p. 57). Thus interaction with a librarian becomes a symbol for interaction with librarianship, and everything about that interaction, including the visual cues, is part of that symbol. "We risk losing the engagement of potential lifelong users of libraries if we fail to present ourselves as welcoming, accessible, engaged, and savvy" (Pagowsky and Rigby, 2014, para. 13). But in addition to this, Brannon (2005) explains that Steele and Aronson's (1995) stereotype threat tells us negative stereotypes affect people in a stereotyped group. "They [Steele and Aronson] proposed that people feel threatened in situations in which they believe their performance will identify them as examples of the group's negative stereotypes." This is called stereotype threat "because the presence of negative stereotypes threatens performance and self-concept. Even if the person does not believe the stereotype or accept that it applies, the threat of being identified with a negative stereotype can be an ever-present factor that puts a person in the spotlight and creates tension and anxiety about performance" (Brannon, 2005, p. 158). Clearly stereotypes about librarian ineptness can be dangerous even when we know we are anything but inept; just because we know that doesn't mean the public knows that.

"Although the value of our work should take the spotlight, when librarian stereotypes have a strong presence, they activate heuristics, or mental shortcuts, for defining what librarians do" (Pagowsky and Rigby, 2014, para. 9). When people don't know what it is we can do for them at the library, they fill in the blanks based on what they have learned from stereotypes; filling in the blanks includes personality and physical characteristics. It seems letting people know what we do is a large part of the problem. Roberto (2014) tells us "library work is often found to lack a sense of cohesion, also known as a 'shared vision' in corporate speak" ("Putting the Pieces Back Together," para. 1). Lacking a shared vision, a sense of cohesion, makes it difficult to educate people about what librarians are and what they do because there is no clear focus of the message. No clear focus means everyone is getting different, possibly conflicting, messages, and this confusion will lead people to fall back on stereotypes. This suggests that we need to both improve people's knowledge about what we do as well as combat stereotypes about our image; they must be done in tandem because they are two sides of the same coin, and that coin is providing the public with an accurate picture of librarianship so it feels comfortable with and eager to utilize library services.

Scenarios like the one in Bloomsburg and the overlooked consequences of stereotype threat are exactly why we need to continue understanding the stereotypes held about the profession; however, knowing what stereotypes are out there is not enough. We must go beyond the focus of literature thus far — telling us what people think about us — and consider how these thoughts impact our ability to do our jobs, how we can change these stereotypes (if it's even possible to change them), and where these stereotypes come from (i.e. what psychological, historical, and cultural influences have led to these stereotypes). It is only with a deeper understanding of stereotypes that we can strategically think about what aspects of the stereotypes are possible to change in the near future and what aspects of the stereotypes may take generations to change.

CHAPTER 2

Librarianship's Historical Influence on Stereotypes

This chapter provides a brief history of the library profession. It is not a comprehensive history; instead it emphasizes moments that highlight the roots of some of our current library and librarian stereotypes.

Gray (2012) discusses librarians and their identity, noting that the current identity crisis stems from history and the historical development of the profession. In fact Gray tells readers "the initiation of some defining aspects of the profession" are seen in "the examples of individuals involved with the library of Alexandria," and adds "it is possible to trace the origins of many of the skills that 'librarians' of today in fact recognize as being classic facets of the profession's identity, such as cataloguing, indexing, and classification" to Alexandria (p. 38). Both the great library and the smaller library at Alexandria were founded in the third century B.C., and we still perform these same core functions, albeit in different ways. The libraries were also geared toward scholars as opposed to the public, so it was easy to see how libraries were associated solely with learning and scholars as opposed to the average person. Battles (2003) also tells us that while the librarians did face budgetary concerns, their goal was for the library to hold everything; essentially it was meant to be a repository of items for scholars (p. 30). Thus as far back as the third century B.C. the profession encouraged the development of its stereotypes as a place for scholars and a repository for knowledge. It wasn't until the Renaissance that the concept of a true public library came about.

Prior to the Renaissance, the rise of Islam led to a flourishing of libraries. Battles (2003) notes that during the rise of Islam, "the first Umayyad Caliph, Muawiyah I, appointed a *sahib al-masahif,* or curator of books, to care for his royal library" in Damascus (p. 62). This curator of books was the predecessor of library keepers and librarians, and the title "curator of books" implies the stereotypes that all librarians do is organize and manage books.

Centuries later, in 1694, Richard Bentley was appointed Keeper of the Royal Library in England. His goal was to turn the library "into an international institution of higher learning" (Battles, 2003, p. 93). His vision of the library was ahead of its time, as was his vision of what a librarian should be professionally; Bentley believed a librarian should do more than just oversee books. "He firmly felt that the work of finding, keeping, and organizing a scholarly collection of books was essential to modern scholarship, and that the keeping of libraries should be entrusted to people whose intellectual development was strong and unhindered. The dominant opinion, however, was different" (Battles, 2003, p. 113). The dominant opinion was that the library keepers simply organized and managed books.

In the 1600s and 1700s, the library world faced a debacle similar to the one it faces today — how much should libraries change, and how much should they remain unchanged? What was best for loyal patrons, and what reflected the changing attitudes of society? Bentley found himself amidst this debate about whether the library's collection should consist primarily of religious texts and other traditional library materials or whether the collection should also include the newer secular works and formats; those who campaigned for the traditional collection were known as "ancients" while those who campaigned for change, this included Bentley, were known as "modernists." The "most enduring picture of the quarrel of the ancients and the moderns" was depicted by Jonathan Swift (an ancient who later became a modernist) in his 1704 story *A full and true account of the battle fought last Friday between the ancient and the modern books in St. James's library,* better known as *The Battle of the Books* (Battles, 2003, p. 96).

Because Bentley was a modernist, Swift targeted him for satire. Bentley's character in the story humiliated himself in the first battle and "tried to avenge himself by installing the ancients' enemies in the 'fairest apartments' of the library, while burying the ancients and their 'advocates' to the dusky corners, and threatening that 'upon the least displeasure' they will be 'turned out of doors.' But the keeper of the books couldn't keep his books straight — for there arose 'a strong confusion of place among all the books in the library.'" (Battles, 2003, p. 102). Battles (2003) tells us this depiction "may have offered the first instance of that literacy cliché — the doddering library" because "all the stereotypes are in motion: the learned pedant, crabbed and dust-addled, himself consumed by and among consuming bookworms, is lost in the vastness of the library" (p. 103). Swift's depiction not only presents the doddering librarian, but it also presents its accompanying stereotype that still lingers today — the incompetent librarian.

While the library profession was engaged in a battle in England, it was taking root in the U.S. The U.S. library profession originated at Harvard College in 1667 when Samuel Stoddard became the library keeper. Stoddard and later library keepers held the position for short periods of time. It wasn't until James Winthrop was appointed in 1672 that library keeper became a career; Winthrop stayed there for 30 years (Dickinson, 2002, p. 99). Early American library jobs were not glamorous, and collection access was highly restricted. For example, at Harvard the library keepers were required to demand the return of all books once per month for inventory count purposes; also, at the end of his term, the library keeper was responsible to "make good" financially — to pay out of his own pocket — for all unreturned items (Dickinson, 2002, p. 99). It is clear to see why Keer and Carlos (2014) tell us, "The original librarian stereotype, which was superseded by the introduction of his prudish sister, was that of the fussy (white) male curmudgeon" ("Librarian Stereotypes," para. 1). It is also easy to see how this fussy male curmudgeon morphed into the library policeman stereotype we have today — the obsession with order and paying fines as well as a heavily guarded collection were all part of the profession that became part of the stereotype. Thus regardless of gender, the profession did not get off to a patron-friendly, respectable start.

Keer and Carlos (2014) also tell us that early American librarians were almost exclusively from the New England gentility; however, by the mid-1870s this educated class was falling out of favor in the eyes of the American public. After the Civil War, the "self-made man" emerged as the masculine ideal. Gentility "became more identified with old-fashioned values and with femininity" ("Librarianship as a Profession," paras. 4-6). Thus before women entered librarianship, the profession was already being associated with femininity and was afforded less respect by virtue of the men who occupied the positions. It is interesting to note that although the profession began to be devalued because of these men, the devaluing of the profession and its association with femininity is typically blamed solely on women entering the profession.

The mid-1870s also saw the birth of public libraries in the United States; however library history often overlooks this event. In fact Scott (1986) called this a "great gap" in library history, adding, "In 1933 the American Library Association apparently announced that 75 percent of the public libraries then in existence owed their creation to women — yet, except for an old article written by Mois Coit Tyler, none of the standard works in library history so much as mentioned this fact" (p. 400). Thus our own professional history favors the work of men. This also reflects the debate of "large libraries/librarianship" (academic and more prestigious libraries) versus "small libraries/librarianship" (public and less prestigious libraries) happening internally now. Our profession seems to internally value large libraries more than small libraries, and this is reflected in the public's values as well.

Public libraries grew out of women's associations. Scott (1986) explains that there were college-educated women who desired more knowledge and education despite society's lack of encouragement for educating women. In order to obtain this knowledge and education, many formed these associations. "As early as 1800 the first women's voluntary associations had appeared in New England in the shape of benevolent societies…From the very beginning women's associations exhibited a strong tendency toward self-improvement…Tiny benevolent societies formed lending libraries, first for their members and then, gradually, for the whole community" (p. 402).

By the 1870s, the number of women's societies had grown drastically; in fact one kind of organization, "the literary culture club," grew the fastest. If towns with these clubs already had public libraries, the club members were "the most active group of patrons." Some associations "existed for the express purpose of creating public libraries. The prototype may have been the Ladies Library Association of Ann Arbor, Michigan, where as early as 1866 thirty-five women joined together, taxed themselves, rented a room, chose books that members could use free, and any member of the community could borrow for ten cents. By the 1890s innumerable clubs were trying to create public libraries" (Scott, 1986, 402-403).

Scott attributes this stereotypically gendered library development to women's ties to public education, pointing out that early on women looked beyond educating themselves to educating the community (p. 404). While this is in part true — women did look beyond themselves for the good of the community — that was not the original intent of forming women's associations with lending libraries. The original intent was to subvert the system that severely limited their abilities to obtain more education and to do it in a way that seemed appropriate for their gender. Thus by leaving out an important piece of library history, the literature has left out an important piece of women's history. This piece shows women using the system to beat the system as opposed to showing the caring women who put others first. This could have been intentionally left out of history in order to maintain gender stereotypes, or it could have been unintentionally left out of history because librarianship itself favors, and seems to have always favored, large librarianship; the favored side of the profession naturally would have received more attention. Yet considering the fact that large librarianship was and is predominantly male, it's difficult to ignore the fact that these two points are intertwined to create a history and a culture that favors men over women and views the history created by men as more important than the history created by women.

The 1870s were also important for academic libraries — the academic research movement in American universities began in 1876 with the founding of Johns Hopkins; the research movement coincided with an increase in the number of women obtaining higher education and desiring jobs. The American Library Association, which Melville Dewey helped to found, also held its first meeting in 1876. Librarians at this meeting were concerned about their changing roles due to changing technology and changing collections: "Previously, the extent and nature of collections was pretty well understood: it was part of the cultural patrimony handed down from antiquity. But now new kinds of books were being produced, as publishers took advantage of cheap paper and mass production methods to reach out and create new readers for their wares. The reform-minded librarians wished to interpose themselves between the masses and the books, to provide guidance in appropriate kinds of reading" (Battles, 2003, p. 140). Yet Dewey was not a reform-minded librarian — he believed the librarian's role was subordinate to the scholar. Thus when Dewey created the first library school at Columbia College in 1887, and what other schools did when they followed his example, was not to advance women's professionalism but instead "was to limit admissions to the programs to the kind of persons acceptable to the profession" in Dewey's eyes (Shiflett, 2000, p. 256).

Dewey and others were quick to hire women to fill library positions "because they generally worked for lower wages than their male counterparts, and the work assigned to them was almost certainly the dull and more routine tasks that once filled the male librarians' day… Employing women in libraries was also viewed by many as a natural extension of the supposedly inherent feminine qualities of spirituality, housekeeping, and a willingness to help others" (Dickinson, 2002, p. 103-104). While this natural extension of their stereotypical gender qualities may have been one part of the impetus to hire women, Dewey's biographer adds that Dewey encouraged women's entry into the profession "to define the profession down. Women were already socially subordinate to the men who filled faculty roles; for Dewey, this subordination nicely mirrored the professional subordination of librarians to professors and other experts — subordination he deemed necessary to the efficient workings of the library" (Battles, 2003, p. 144-145).

Thus instead of the career becoming more prestigious and valued because of the research movement in universities, the exploitation of cheap female labor led to the field being even more devalued and not taken seriously. The female gender and its consequences were used as a symbol of subordination; after all, at the time women were entering the profession, they were still expected to quit their jobs for marriage and family life so their positions had to be of little value and had to be expendable. Also, the male librarian stereotype became more feminized because male librarians who did not climb the administrative ranks were doing what was now seen as women's work.

While the male librarian stereotype became more feminized, the entrance of women into the profession also led to the gendered division of labor we still see in libraries today — women were assigned more menial, mundane tasks than men while men were in administrative positions overseeing these tasks. This division of labor combined with men's longer amount of time in the workforce and their permanence in the workplace paved the way for men to advance within the field and for women to remain static. However even without their work history and permanence in the workplace, "Christine Williams, sociologist and professor at UT Austin, states, 'Men take their gender privilege with them when they enter predominantly female occupations: this translates into an advantage in spite of numerical rarity'" (as cited in Pho & Masland, 2014, "Complexities and Definitions of Diversity," para. 3). This ability for men to ascend, often quickly, in the ranks of female-dominated fields is known as the glass escalator; this is in contrast to the glass ceiling, which is the barrier that keeps women from advancing in professions. It's possible the glass escalator can be attributed to stereotypes and cultural peer pressure related to traditional male and female jobs. In the case of librarianship, people expect women to be librarians and because of this, along with the stereotype that women are perceived as more caring than men, people may be more likely to approach women working in libraries even if these women are not librarians. Thus the men must be moved to where society tells us they should fit — in an administrative position overseeing women who work with the public as opposed to working with the public themselves. In fact Gaines (2014) tells us, "As the profession became viewed more as a 'woman's job,' men in the profession became viewed as those who failed in more traditionally masculine fields. Librarianship was seen as the last bastion of hope for men. Because of this, and because of the low salaries in librarianship, men often aspired to administrative positions; not only would the compensation be higher, but the intellectual rigor of administration was thought to be more suitably challenging (and more akin to that of male-dominated professions) than positions such as reference, which were considered to be less stimulating" (para. 25). The glass escalator, and to an extent the glass ceiling, may also be impacted by the stereotypical communication styles of men and women — men are traditionally nurtured to communicate for dominance while women are traditionally nurtured to communicate for connections; dominance and competition are more valued in American society and business than are connections.

The history of women dominating the library profession continues today, as does the gendered division of labor. "Of the 118,666 credentialed librarians surveyed in 2009–2010, 98,273, or 82.8 percent, were women;" however, "an Association of Research Libraries survey in 2010 found that, while only 17.2 percent of the librarians were men, they held 40 percent of the director positions in university libraries" (Gaines, 2014, paras. 10, 24). It's no wonder librarianship has, and continues to be, considered a "pink-collar job." Gaines tell us pink-collar jobs "are now defined as those jobs dominated by women, and are considered to bring with them less social status and pay than other jobs [requiring comparable education]. Even though these fields require professional education, many people still hold stereotyped views of those who work in them" (para. 2). As long as the pink-collar label exists and as long as stereotypes about pink-collar jobs exist, librarianship will struggle to attract more men and will struggle to be seen as more than a female profession.

CHAPTER 3

Librarian Stereotypes

Prior to any discussion about stereotypes and their impacts on the profession, we must start with an overview of the popular stereotype categories the literature has already defined. Seale's (2008) stereotype categories are most often cited in the literature. According to Seale, there are five major categories that librarian stereotypes fall into — old maid, policeman, librarian as parody, inept librarian, and hero/heroine librarian. Seale says, "The Old Maid Librarian is perhaps the most common stereotype of librarians found in the mass media" ("Old Maid Librarian," para. 1). The old maids are frumpy, sexless, introverted, and are never seen as fun and exciting people or characters. The old maid stereotype probably grew out of the characteristics expected of the perfect librarian as well as the cultural ideal that women only worked until they were married. According to Attebury (2010), "One hundred years ago, Keller outlined the characteristics of the mythical ideal librarian. Among her qualities were a neat appearance, cordial manner, avoidance of alcohol, drugs, tobacco, gambling, profanity and vulgarity, and deserving of the description, 'wonderfully adaptable, besides being omnipotent, omniscient, omnipresent, and always working overtime at something with superhuman energy and enthusiasm.'" Attebury adds, "Early in the development of U.S. librarianship, the idea of complete allegiance to the library system required of librarians met little resistance from a society that already demanded a woman choose between a career and a family. Thus, it was a short step from Keller's enthusiastic ideal librarian who devoted herself to the job with such alacrity to the stereotype of the Old Maid who had devoted herself perhaps too much, to the point she missed out on other more social aspects of life…Thus at some point, a transformation occurred from Keller's ideal librarian, which in actuality is still a fairly positive image, into derision toward unmarried spinster librarians" (pp. 2-3). While Keller's ideal librarian appears to be a positive image, one cannot help but wonder if this description actually invites the spinster old maid stereotype; after all, when a job description calls for you to devote your life to the profession, regardless of gender, the underlying assumption is that the job is your life. Perhaps the ideal librarian was, at that time, a woman destined to be a spinster; surely someone who only saw her job as something temporary until she married would not put such effort into it that she would ignore the social aspects of life that would enable her to meet her future husband.

  The old maid stereotype doesn't have an old man counterpart — men instead are sometimes depicted as feminine and gay, but that depiction was not widespread enough for Seale to give it a category. Men do have the policeman stereotype. The policeman librarian is a feared stereotype — policeman librarians dole out the punishment and take no mercy. "The power and authority of the librarian is directly bound up with his/her knowledge. The main characteristics of the policeman librarian can thus be seen as the possession of authority and/or knowledge and the ability to act on it" (Seale, 2008, "Policeman Librarian," para. 2). The policeman librarian stereotype likely grew from the original role of the library keeper. The librarian as parody stereotype is a stereotype that makes fun of these ridiculous stereotypes. By exaggerating the qualities of stereotypes, we can see how ridiculous they are. The inept librarian is a librarian who either is too incompetent to do his or her job well or who dreads actually doing his or her job and would rather not work with patrons. Finally, Seale gives us the hero/heroine librarian — the librarian who saves the day either through outrageous adventures or while performing seemingly mundane tasks that are in fact patron advocacy tasks: "These portrayals…depict their work as fundamentally important" (Seale, 2008, "Hero/ine Librarian").

Attebury (2010) conducted a study in which she examined the depictions of librarians in YouTube videos created by both librarians and non-librarians and came across three other dominant stereotypes — the psycho librarian, the sexy librarian, and the occupation as "fun and positive" (p. 5). The psycho librarian stereotype results from the library policeman stereotype being taken too far. The sexy librarian is a librarian who is pretty but conservative. Once she — it is always a woman — breaks free of her conservative nature, she is a bombshell beauty who wants sex. By 2010, Attebury found that the sexy librarian was replacing the old maid: "Ironically the Old Maid depictions of librarians, while common throughout American history and still occasionally found in YouTube videos, seems to have been surpassed by…the sexy librarian, or even the sexy old maid" (p. 3). Poulin (2008) previously made a similar observation: as far back as 1999, "negative characteristics like wearing hair in a bun and shushing patrons have virtually disappeared from the screen" (Beth Yeagley, 1999, as cited in Poulin, p. 3). The profession as "fun and positive" stereotype shows libraries as fun, valuable places to be and shows viewers librarians aren't "shushers." Attebury and Poulin were both only examining YouTube videos and not all media, so this could have impacted their results; however their results deserve attention because YouTube videos are created by the public so they give insight into what the public thinks about the profession as opposed to what traditional media tell the public to think about the profession.

Although Seale's original major stereotype categories and Attebury's later additions have become the most popular mentioned in the library literature, other stereotypes exist. In fact before Seale introduced her categories, Posner (2000) introduced us to the "know it all" librarian who reveled in showing off his or her "intellectual grandeur" (p. 113). More recently, Mizra and Seale (2011) introduced the gatekeeper stereotype. They use the examples of Rupert Giles from the *Buffy the Vampire Slayer* television series, Flynn Carson from *The Librarian* movies, and Henry DeTamble from *The Time Traveler's Wife* book to explain how the gatekeeper is an updated version of the profession's library keeper. Like the library keepers, gatekeepers are male, enforce the rules, and maintain order; however, unlike the library keepers, gatekeepers are respected for their power, knowledge, and masculinity. "This masculinity, however, is not the masculinity of John Wayne or Dirty Harry; it is a combination of dominant Generation X models of masculinity that acknowledges the impact of feminism but ultimately seeks to reify male power in a post-feminist age" (p. 143). Mizra and Seale go on to tell us these gatekeepers "confront the irrational as embedded in the paranormal elements of these texts; however, these male librarians are all able to control the paranormal, even if only to a degree. Unlike female librarians, burdened by the domestic and the bodily and dominated by the rationality of the library, these male librarian gatekeepers are to be admired. They are manly, powerful, and they act for the forces of good; they are cool" (p. 145). These gatekeepers represent the gender divisions in our society and in the profession that are still prevalent — men are in control of the library and its power, men are the rational people controlling the irrational women. Also, these men have roles that are "manly," "cool," and "powerful" — these are attributes society values. Female librarians do not have any comparable gatekeeper stereotypes that command respect and are seen as "cool" or "powerful."

There are two other contemporary stereotypes that appear in writings about the profession — the hipster librarian and the tattooed librarian. Both of these stereotypes carry positive and negative connotations. The hipster image paints the profession as just that — hip, fun, and something the younger generation is embracing. In 2007, Jesella's *New York Times* article described librarians as "a hipper crowd of shushers," and her article went on to describe how the profession and librarians were the complete opposite of boring old maids. Later, when describing the 2013 American Library Association annual conference and its attendees, Borrelli (2013) said, "The librarian of the future (and, arguably, the present) — judging by the 'I Love Free Speech' T-shirts, piercings, and tattoos on the younger librarians attending the conventions — is not a shusher, but a hipster, only more tolerable" (para. 24). While the tattoos in this case get lumped in with the hipster crowd, tattooed librarians may or may not describe themselves as hipsters. Pappas (2014) tells us a Harris Interactive survey showed approximately 20% of American adults have tattoos ("Introduction," para. 1). With this increasing prevalence of tattoos in society, it would seem natural to expect librarians to have them as well; this societal phenomenon shouldn't be special enough to warrant a stereotype. However it seems librarians think this is a way to draw attention from the old maid stereotype. For example, in 2013 the Rhode Island Library Association's fundraising plans included "the launch of the first ever Tattooed Librarians of the Ocean State 2014 Calendar" (Mehrer, 2013, para. 1). The project was "designed to change perceptions of the library profession, while also highlighting vital library and information services available in many types of libraries" (Mehrer,

2013, para. 4). In 2014, Pappas conducted a survey of a group of tattooed librarians. Of the 171 respondents, only 28% said yes there was something special about being a tattooed librarian while 79% said no there wasn't anything special about it and 2% had ambiguous feelings. While fewer thought there was anything special about it, "stereotypes were mentioned twice as often" when the "yes" group explained their response as when the "no" group explained their responses. Specifically, "the negation of stereotypes was a more common and explicit theme. Note here the contrast set is between the speaking individual and the imagined 'other' who is almost always described as an older, uptight, sexless spinster" ("Making Narratives, Enacting Agency").

The stereotypes discussed thus far have positive and negative connotations; they are not just negative. "Stereotypes may indicate a shared group identity resultant from similar experiences and also a desire to be part of the 'in-group.' For example, a librarian might deliberately yet unnecessarily don a pair of glasses so as to appear more bookish or intellectual and to fit in with peers of a similar nature…Problems with stereotypes arise when a person fails to realize that categories are made up of individuals who are not exactly identical…Stereotypes are even more problematic when they cease functioning as mere categories and are used as the basis for judgment that has a real-life impact on the unique individuals in the category" (Attebury, 2010, pp. 1-2).

Unfortunately too many librarian stereotypes are negative and are based on outmoded ideas of what librarians do. This impacts the profession both internally and externally: "The effects of occupational stereotypes have more impact than simply making people feel proud or embarrassed about the profession. The potential exists for stereotypes to impact public support and compensation for the profession" (Attebury,

2010, p. 8). Stereotypes that conjure up the scene of a technologically inept librarian stamping books leads to the cries of the death of libraries and librarianship, and this impacts respect and consequently funding for the profession. A lack of funding, particularly on the part of public libraries, may lead to the elimination of programs and services that are vital for the growth, education, and success of community members. Stereotypical images of the library policeman or the shushing old maid giving you an evil look over the top of her glasses don't encourage patrons to approach librarians, and this may mean that people who need help finding important information will not get the help and will not find the information they need. And the stereotype of this being a female profession lowers the salary and level of prestige afforded the profession in addition to discouraging men and some women from entering the profession.

However, Poulin (2008) says, "Recent literature seems to indicate that there is an increasingly higher percentage of positive images of librarianship in television and film. The 2007 documentary *The Hollywood Librarian* presented dozens of clips of feature films that illustrate the wide array of portrayals of librarians, both positive and negative. These clips were interwoven with interviews with a number of actual librarians in an attempt to shed greater light upon what professionals in the field are accomplishing on a daily basis" (p. 2).

Despite these images, Pagowsky and DeFrain (2014) point out the hot versus cold bind that librarians face. People tend to favor those whom they perceive as warm as opposed to those whom they perceive as cold despite actual job competency; however, the authors cite a study from Cuddy, Glick, and Benninger (2011) that describes "implications of warmth versus competence traits, noting that mutual exclusivity really only affects women — an effect which is magnified in a woman-dominated profession." Essentially, Cudddy, Glick, and Benniger's study says that women — not men — are caught in a "double bind in which being judged as high on one dimension leads to lower judgments on the other" (as cited in Pagowsky & DeFrain, 2014, "What is 'Warm' and What is 'Cold'?," para. 4). This presents a problem considering librarianship isn't just a stereotypically female-dominated profession but it is also a field that requires public interaction. If we are perceived as cold, people will not want to approach us. If we are perceived as warm, people will want to approach us. But if we are perceived as warm and by extension incompetent, will people really want to approach us? Why approach someone who is incompetent? In media depictions with the old maid stereotype, her intelligence is never called into question; however she is also *not* depicted as friendly and approachable. While the intelligence of the sexy librarian has never been called into question either, we saw these librarians in early films leave the profession for marriage so we didn't see them as serious librarians even if we didn't explicitly see them as incompetent.

While the double bind applies to women, it does not apply to men. In the real world, men can be cold and competent or warm and competent; however, in stereotypical librarian depictions, men are often depicted as incompetent regardless of whether or not they are warm and goofy or just plain mean. When men are depicted as mean, their attitude overshadows their competence, or lack thereof. It's interesting to see how a profession that is deemed a low status female profession is at the same time depicted as something for which you need to be intelligent to do, and which the more highly esteemed gender cannot competently complete.

Pagowsky and DeFrain (2014) also tell us another way the stereotypical old maid image harms the profession: "Librarianship being dominated by women and falling into an older demographic equates with two major identities that Cuddy, Glick, and Benninger categorize as invoking pity" — women and the elderly ("What is 'Warm' and What is 'Cold'?," para. 5). Groups that invoke pity are "low-status, noncompetitive groups perceived as warm but incompetent" (Cuddy, Glick, & Benninger, 2011, as cited in Pagowsky and DeFrain, 2014, "What is 'Warm' and What is 'Cold'?," para. 5). Pagowski and DeFrain say this pity is passively harmful to those groups; the harm is passive because people neglect the groups.

Admittedly librarians were reactive in dealing with their image and its impact on the profession. Their "noncompetitive" nature, their nature that allows them to stay in the background and serve patrons without the desire for special recognition, hurt the profession rather than helping people to see it as an admirable profession that requires skill because the stereotypes already situated the profession in a view of pity. Interestingly, the view of pitying librarians seems to stem from their former old maid status as opposed to their low pay and low professional status. Women who are intelligent and who dedicate their lives to a career that demands intelligence were pitied and used as a scare tactic at a time when it was thought that the natural path for all women was to give up work for marriage; thus successful career women were held up as examples of something women should not aspire to be because the old maid status trumped the successful career woman status. The "What if?" scene in *It's a Wonderful Life* is a prime example of this. If Mary Bailey's husband George hadn't been around, she would have been doomed to be an old maid librarian; this was such a terrible fate that it convinced George not to commit suicide. She is not praised for the fact that without a husband she would've had a stable career that provided a paycheck.

Radford and Radford (1997) extend this idea of pity and add, "The librarian stereotype does not exist in a cultural vacuum, of course. It meshes with portrayals and literary uses of the library institution. In the western literary tradition, the library represents a place of peace and order and has been seen as a metaphor for rationality" (p. 254). They tell us the librarian is guarding materials from the irrational others who seek to disrupt this order, and say that the librarian is actually controlling discourse (rather than encouraging the free exchange of ideas and access to information to democratize knowledge) and she "guards against the possible danger of uncontrolled discourse through complex mechanisms of order: indexes, catalogs, controlled vocabularies, and retrieval systems" (p. 260). Radford and Radford also question why someone who is a gatekeeper of order and knowledge is not afforded respect, but they ultimately come to the conclusion that the female librarian is just a front — she isn't feared and afforded respect but is instead being manipulated and used to control discourse so the dominant discourse remains dominant; however she is "only a woman" and isn't feared, so people don't realize discourse is being controlled. If people realized this, there could be chaos as they try to unlock hidden knowledge. "The stereotype of the female librarian is ultimately one of a victim. Female librarians are not gods who create and control the overpowering rationality of the library's space of knowledge. The stereotype is a front that defuses the power and fear of this rationality. Indeed the relationship between rationality and the librarian is reversed in the female stereotype: it is the rationality that creates and controls the librarian...such figures are to be pitied rather than revered or admired" (p. 261).

Radford and Radford's views of the female librarian who appears to be controlling discourse but is actually being manipulated by the dominant group is an interesting parallel to gender studies concepts. In earlier times in history, and even still to some extent today, women were seen as irrational and emotional while men were the rational, reserved gender; thus it seems strange that a stereotypically irrational group of people should be charged with maintaining so much rational order. And despite being charged with maintaining rationality and order, women are still afforded low status and respect. But if we look at who controls the female librarians, we find that historically and still today men are primarily the supervisors; thus the men are controlling rationality and are imposing it on women. Rather than women being manipulated to keep the dominant discourse dominant, they are actually being manipulated to keep the dominant sex dominant. In either case, the woman is still a figure to be pitied.

While it is easy to spot blatantly negative stereotypes, it's difficult to see how stereotypes that seem positive can in fact be negative. The earlier discussion of Keller's ideal librarian, which was positive on the surface, carried connotations that led to the old maid stereotype. Similarly the seemingly positive stereotypes of the hipster librarian and the tattooed librarian may end up leading to negative thoughts. How can something that shows librarians as hip and fun be bad? The term "hipster" has come to have a negative connotation. Ferrier (2014) tells us "what was once an umbrella term for a counter-culture tribe of young creative types…has morphed into a pejorative term for people who looked, lived, and acted a certain way" (para. 3). As the trend to be hip, progressive, and against the cultural grain became common and commercialized, the term "hipster" took on a negative connotation. Tattoos also carry a negative connotation.

Although approximately 20% of American adults have tattoos, "they are still generally read as indicators of deviance" (Pappas, 2014, "Introduction," para. 1). Visible tattoos often lead to debates about how professional, or typically how unprofessional, they make someone look. Tattoos can also carry different meanings for different people and may make some patrons uncomfortable.

Various librarian representations show these stereotypes, and the literature examines many of these representations. For example, Radford and Radford (2003) look at Mary in the movie *Party Girl*, and countless books and articles make reference to Mary Bailey's debacle in *It's a Wonderful Life* and to Marion the librarian in *The Music Man*. Kneale (2009) examines librarian depictions across all types of media, Tevis and Tevis (2005) look at librarians in cinema, Burns (1998) composed a bibliography of librarian representations in all forms of fiction, Kniffel (2005) discusses Flynn Carsen in *The Librarian*, and Seale (2008) gives examples of librarian depictions that fit her stereotype categories. This list is by no means comprehensive, but it provides an example of how much has been written on specific librarian representations. While these authors tend to look at depictions through the lens of one particular stereotype, some depictions may represent multiple stereotypes. Rupert Giles from *Buffy the Vampire Slayer* is one librarian character who has received mixed reactions in the literature and who does not fit neatly into one stereotype category. DeCandido (1999) claims Giles "has done more for the image of the profession than anything in the past 50 years, with the possible exception of Katherine Hepburn in *Desk Set*. Giles, this wiley and attractive professional, is our hero librarian: a pop culture idol whose love of books and devotion to research hold the key to saving the universe" (p. 44). DeCandido admits he "moves across the stereotype in other, not necessarily positive ways — he is both male and technologically inept" (p. 44) but ultimately he is a positive image because he is portrayed as a hardworking researcher whose research saves the day. "While snide comments abound, the core belief that knowledge is the answer underlies all" (p. 46). Thus DeCandido sees Giles as both a hero librarian and a sexy librarian. Cullen (2000) has a very different opinion of Giles and even refers to him as a "professional image slayer" (p. 42). Cullen believes Giles to be an inept librarian: "He is a Luddite working in a field that is reliant on information technology. He is self-absorbed and unhelpful…He has no concept of reader service and is always surprised when students enter the library to do real research" (p. 42). Giles represents yet another stereotype, too. Mizra and Seale (2011) describe him as a gatekeeper whose role is to protect people from harmful knowledge — Giles protects people from information about the occult and only reveals it to Buffy as necessary. Mizra and Seale tell us representations of Giles, as well as Flynn Carson and Henry DeTamble, "work to construct them as powerful, authoritative, and masculine gatekeepers, whose role in limiting access to knowledge is necessary in order to control the irrational, and implicitly, the female, as embodied in paranormal elements in these texts" (p. 136). Giles becomes a father figure to Buffy and believes his duties to protect her are more important than his duties as a librarian. These gatekeepers "derive power and authority from their knowledge, their ability to regulate the flow of knowledge, the rationality ascribed to them by their positions as librarians, and their modified but still potent masculinity. Their control over knowledge is depicted as altruistic and paternal" (p. 144).

    Clearly librarian depictions, just like real-life librarians, do not fit exclusively into one stereotype category. In fact the more analyzing you do, the more you realize these characters can be very multifaceted; this is the case with Giles. It is interesting and troubling that our profession cannot even agree on whether or not a depiction represents a positive or a negative stereotype. Is it any wonder we have trouble fighting stereotypes, then? The battle over whether or not Giles is a positive or negative librarian representation provides a glimpse at the internal divisions that exist within the profession and create an "us versus them" mentality that must be overcome in order to combat stereotypes.

CHAPTER 4

Culture and Theories Impacting Stereotype Development

Stereotype creation and perpetuation is no easy concept to understand. Theories related to it are rooted in many areas of study, particularly psychology, sociology, communication, literature, and gender studies, but it's impossible to have a discussion about any kind of stereotypes and related theories without acknowledging that cultural context greatly shapes them. One important aspect of culture to keep in mind while reading this chapter is the idea of nature versus nurture. Does our nature (i.e. our biology, the way we are created) impact our actions (i.e. Are women born with certain traits and are men born with certain traits?) or does our nurture (i.e. the way a family raises a child) impact our actions (i.e. Do boys and girls learn their gender-specific traits, or do they learn to defy gender-specific traits, from what they are taught?). This author's opinion is that nurture is more responsible than nature for actions, although she believes it's impossible to deny nature and the natural body processes may have some impact on our lives; her thoughts mesh with Myer's (2005) thoughts: "Although biologically influenced, gender is also socially constructed. What biology initiates, culture accentuates" (p. 95).

Culture is so integral to understanding all aspects of the librarian stereotypes and all other theories surrounding it that it's impossible to contain discussion of it in a single chapter. It's also impossible to isolate cultural studies from the other areas of study. While this chapter has in-depth discussions of different subjects separated into sections, there is some overlap between the sections, and these concepts also appear throughout the rest of the book.

Culture and Cultural Studies

The field of cultural studies examines the ways people are shaped by the culture of their environment. This "shaping" permeates all aspects of our lives — our thoughts, actions, morals, values, manner of speech, etc. Stephen Littlejohn says cultural studies utilizes two definitions of the term "culture": (1) "the common ideas on which a society or group rests, its ideology, or the collective ways by which a group understands its experience," and (2) "the practices or the entire way of life of a group — what individuals do materially from day to day" (as cited in Radford and Radford, 2003, p. 55). Nanda and Warms (2009) tell us "anthropologists have long proposed that culture is a shared mental model that people use to organize, to classify, and ultimately to understand the world" (p. 28). Thus a culture is a shared group experience that provides the group with a shared frame of reference for how things in life are or should be. This shared frame of reference helps to create and perpetuate stereotypes. Stereotypes can become so ingrained in culture that it takes a major cultural shift to change a way of thinking, and even then remnants of the stereotypes may be lurking in the background. Gender studies illustrates this interplay of culture and stereotypes — for centuries, women were seen as different than men, as people who were fit to be wives and mothers as their careers. While our culture has shifted and women are valuable members of the workforce outside of the home, we still see women fighting for equal pay, we still see traditionally and/or predominantly female professions devalued, and we still expect females to be the primary child caregivers.

Anderson (1988) tells us "culture provides prescriptions for social behavior;" unfortunately "one feature of a culture is that its members come to take cultural patterns for granted. Thus, culture provides its members with tacit knowledge; much of what they believe as true or what they perceive as real is learned to the point where it is no longer questioned. Culture provides assumptions that often go unexamined but that, nonetheless, fundamentally guide our behavior and our beliefs" (p. 74). These assumptions may lead to stereotypes.

Culture provides us with patterns on which to model our behavior; in fact Bandura's social learning theory says we learn from observing one another and modeling this behavior. Brannon (2005) invokes social learning theory to explain that people learn traditional gender roles based on the traditional roles they see modeled at home (p. 116-117). Social learning theory raises an important question when it comes to people entering heavily stereotypical professions: If we learn and have stereotypes reinforced since birth, then will these careers attract those who are stereotypically suited for them? If that's the case, is the stereotype constantly perpetuating itself and creating a new reality?

The socio-cultural tradition of the field of communication studies takes the point of view that culture shapes language. This tradition is "based on the premise that as people talk, they produce and reproduce culture. Most of us assume that words reflect what actually exists. However, theorists in this tradition suggest the process often works the other way around. Our view of reality is strongly shaped by the language we've used since we were infants" (Griffin, 2006, p. 28). Culture shaping our language, and by extension our view of reality, is why we have gendered language and stereotypes. In fact Sapir and Whorf tell us that reality is shaped by the group's language.

Culture also dictates which discourse is the dominant discourse, and Foucault believes the dominant discourse, or the language system of those in the dominant social group, provides us with the shared frames of reference we use to make sense of the world. This is noticeable in the sports metaphors we use in business, which came about at a time when sports and business were dominated by men; thus these metaphors shaped the business world in accordance with male ideals, and this perhaps kept the dominant discourse dominant because the other social groups didn't have enough knowledge to enter the conversation or change the metaphors.

Hall expands on Foucault's discourse ideas by telling us "the primary function of discourse is to make meaning…To say that two people belong to the same culture is to say that they interpret the world in roughly the same ways and can express themselves, their thoughts and feelings about the world in ways that will be understood by each other" (Griffin, 2006, p. 374).

Because culture shapes discourse, culture will also shape the way we view not just sex differences but also the entire concept of gender. Understanding how ideas about gender are culturally created is critical when considering whether or not a profession viewed as female can ever really break this gender stereotype. Even the idea of a dominant discourse paints the picture of an "us versus them" mentality. This contributes to our binary view of gender in which we have our gender and "the other" gender. However this binary view of gender is cultural. In fact when Europeans came to America, they found many Native American tribes had less rigid gender roles. "More than 130 Native American societies" accepted the idea of berdaches — "men or women who adopted gender-related behaviors of the other gender." For example, "The Zuni saw gender roles as learned rather than fixed by biology. Each gender had a specific role, but individuals were not necessarily tied to that role by their biological sex…some Latin American native cultures had the belief that parents should choose their child's gender, regardless of the child's biological sex" (Brannon, 2005, p. 155). Also, according to Nanda and Warms (2009), Indian society has a third, "ambiguous gender role" known as the hijras. "Although born male, they are considered neither man nor woman." They undergo castration which is seen "as a rebirth, and is carried out as an act of devotion to the Hindu Mother Goddess. After this operation, hijras are believed to incorporate the goddess' power of procreation. Thus, their presence is required at weddings and at the birth of a child." Hijras are born man but undergo castration and "adopt women's clothing, gestures, and behaviors," yet they cannot bear children; thus they are thought of as "not man," "not woman," or "man plus woman" (p. 170-171). Interestingly they have one definition that encompasses both genders in addition to two definitions that promote the idea of "the other." Thus it seems that how you adhere to the genders and roles and how much gender is tied to biology is much more fluid in other cultures. This fluidity impacts how we think and talk about "the other" and how much we value gender roles.

Culture and cultural ideals are created and recreated every day not just through our language, but also through media representations. The reflection hypothesis "assumes the mass media reflect the values of the general population. Images in the media are seen as representing dominant ideals within the population, particularly because of the capitalistic structure. According to Gerbner (1978), the ideals of the population are incorporated into symbolic representations in the media. The reflection hypothesis asserts that, although the media images are make-believe, they do symbolize dominant social beliefs and images" (Andersen, 1988, p. 30). Reflection hypothesis coincides with Foucault's concept of discourse because it shows that the dominant group's ideals are represented.

Andersen (1988) adds, "The values and images of women and men in the media represent some of the most conservative views of women and men. Role-learning theory hypothesizes that sexist and racist images in the media (and the absence thereof) encourage role modeling" (p. 30). Thus culture influences media which in turn reflects and influences culture, and we are caught in a vicious cycle of perpetuating stereotypes.

Clearly culture and cultural ideals permeate every aspect of our lives. While it's impossible to truly separate culture from other theories/aspects relating to stereotypes, these other theories/aspects — communication, gender, and media representations — are explained in more detail in the following sections.

Communication and Language

Through spoken and written language, we communicate our thoughts about the way the world does — or the way we think the world should — work. We also communicate our ideals and what we expect from certain people or certain groups. Literary and communication theories focus on how language shapes our world. The aforementioned nature versus nurture debate mentioned earlier could be extended to language. According to Culler (1997), "How language relates to thought has been a major issue for recent theory. At one extreme is the common-sense view that language just provides the names for thoughts that exist independently; language offers a way of expressing pre-existing thoughts. At the other extreme is the Sapir-Whorf hypothesis named for two linguists who claimed that the language we speak determines what we can think" (p. 58).

Ferdinand de Saussure describes language as a system of arbitrary sign symbols that organize the world. Sandstrom, Martin, and Fine (2010) tell us "a sign is directly connected to an object or event and calls forth a fixed or habitual response. Its meaning is associated with its physical form and can be grasped through the senses. Symbols are something that people create and use to stand for something else…A symbol, then, is any object, gesture, or word that becomes an abstract representation of something else. Whatever it represents constitutes its meaning" (p. 52). For example, the word "cup" leads many of us to think of something we use to drink liquid from, yet it has no connection to the image of something we use to drink liquid from other than the connection we assign it; a cup could just as easily have been called a pen, but we took an object — a symbol — and arbitrarily assigned it meaning, making it a sign. This is why languages can use the exact same word to represent two entirely different things; the word "pan," for example, means something we use for baking in English while in Spanish it means bread. This is also why language evolves as needed, and we have seen the definition and application of words change in addition to new words being created to talk about new ideas. The word "text" is a prime example of the definition and application of words changing. The word has been in existence as a verb since the 1500s, however it wasn't until 1998 that it was used to mean sending a text message via a mobile device (Text, v., 2014). The word "selfie" is an example of a word that was created to talk about a new concept that came about because of technology — the rise of digital cameras that immediately displayed your photo and allowed you to delete it and take it again because it didn't require film to be developed as well as the rise of cellular phones with cameras in the 21st century made it easy and fun to take self portraits or selfies; according to the OED, this word first came into use in 2002 (Selfie, n., 2014). Thus we created a word to be able to discuss a new function of new technology. Self portraits certainly existed before digital cameras and camera phones, but a selfie is a new form of a traditional self portrait that was not widely available before the creation of these devices. If these words, or sign symbols, were fixed, then we would not be able to assign new meaning to them to fit our needs; however, once we arbitrarily assign new meanings to symbols, the meanings tend to stick. Once we have defined something, it becomes our point of reference to which we compare other things. This creates opposites — we define what something is by comparing it to what it is not based on our points of reference. Thus we have a female and we identify her as a female by understanding she is not a male — she does not have a penis or other anatomy that makes her male, so she is the opposite of a male. Saussure also described language as "a system of differences. What makes each element of a language what it is, what gives it its identity, are the contrasts between it and other elements within the system" (Culler, 1997, p. 57). Culler explains, "We don't know who 'we' refers to in this text; only that it is 'we' as opposed to 'I' alone, and to 'he,' 'she,' 'it,' 'you,' and 'they'" (p. 56). Thus our language, if we define things in terms of opposites, ingrains a sense of dichotomy in our culture.

Saussure describes language as a way of expressing pre-existing thoughts — I had a thought and had to choose a symbol to represent it. But University of Chicago linguist Edward Sapir and his student Benjamin Lee Whorf claim that these symbols that are in place will then shape what we think. Saussure said thought comes before the linguistic symbol while Sapir and Whorf say the symbol comes before the thought. "The Sapir-Whorf hypothesis of linguistic relativity states that the structure of a culture's language shapes what people think and do. The 'real world' is to a large extent unconsciously built upon the language habits of the group. Their theory of linguistic relativity counters the assumption that all languages are similar and that words merely act as vehicles to carry meaning" (Griffin, 2006, p. 29). Instead of words simply carrying meaning, words direct meaning by directing how we think. This difference in linguistic structure impacting how and what we think can be seen across cultures and languages. For example, in English we do not assign gender to words to determine which form of "the" to use; we use "the" for all words regardless of whether or not we are talking about a cat or a table, while in Spanish "the" changes to "el" before masculine words and "la" before feminine words — we have "el gato" (the cat) and "la mesa" (the table). The difference is also evident in the pronoun "you" and how we speak to each other. In English, we say "you" regardless of who we are talking to; the phrase, "Do you understand?," is the same regardless of whether or not we are speaking formally (i.e. to a supervisor) or informally (i.e. to a friend). In Spanish, the phrase, "Do you understand?" is different depending on whether you are speaking formally (¿Entiende ud.?) or informally (¿Entiendes tú?). Thus the Spanish language structure compels us to think of the world in terms of gender and formality in a way the English language structure does not.

 Both Saussure's and Sapir and Whorf's theories represent a cultural and linguistic dichotomy. This dichotomy creates a very rigid organization. In addition to his theory, Saussure says that language symbols organize the world. It naturally follows that redefining meanings or allowing symbols to be more fluid can disrupt the organization of the world, or at least the organization of the world of a particular culture — a male entering a stereotypically female profession disrupts our organization of the world because it doesn't conform to our pre-existing symbols of genders.

 While Saussure's and Sapir and Whorf's hypotheses represent dichotomies at either extreme, they couldn't exist without each other. We first need a system of language so we can begin to express ideas, but where does the language come from? What influences our choice of which symbols represent which ideas? Culture provides the context for our language and thought. This is why Nanda and Warms (2009) tell us "language is so heavily freighted with culture that understanding one is almost always key to understanding the other" (p. 79-80). And once we have a language in place to express ideas, this becomes a point of reference and of course will shape how we think and how we express thoughts. "As Anslem Strauss has observed, people act toward objects in light of the names they give to these objects…In naming an object, we classify it and give meaning to it, thereby evaluating it and calling forth action toward it" (Sandstrom, Martin, & Fine, 2010, p. 54). Then the cycle begins again and we are left in a philosophical conundrum akin to, "Which came first, the chicken or the egg?" While it may not be possible to completely determine whether language shapes thoughts or thoughts shape language, it is impossible to deny language and thought are intimately connected and work together to create and perpetuate meaning.

Blumer's symbolic interactionism theory in communication studies examines the interaction of language, thought, and meaning, and how this interaction impacts what people think of themselves and how they fit into their communities. Blumer's theory is built on three premises: 1). "Humans act toward people or things on the basis of the meanings they assign to those people or things," 2). "Meanings arise out of the social interactions that people have with each other. Meaning is negotiated through the use of language, hence the term symbolic interactionism…it's only by talking with others — symbolic interaction — that we come to ascribe meaning and develop a discourse," and 3). "An individual's interpretation of symbols is modified by his or her own thought process"

(Griffin, 2006, p. 56-59). Along with Blumer's second premise is the idea that "the words we use have default assumptions...the subtle tyranny of symbols is that we usually don't consciously think about the mental jump we are making. Unless we're brought up short by some obvious glitch in our taken-for-granted logic...we'll probably assume that the way we think things are is the way they ought to be" (Griffin, 2006, p. 58). These default assumptions come from the expectations our society and our culture place on groups of people. Sandstrom, Martin, & Fine (2010) tell us "much of our socialization consists of learning the common definitions of our society, as well as the roles we are expected to play." They add that as we interact with people, we "place them in social categories that allow us to assess ourselves and others fairly quickly and accurately." Finally, they tell us "being aware of roles, we can disregard many of the personal traits or differences of others as we interact with them, since we can expect them to act in some standardized way as occupants of a given status" (p. 148). Essentially we are subconsciously stereotyping people.

Blumer's premises can easily be applied to stereotypes:

- Premise 1: We act toward people based on the pre-conceive notions (typically stereotypes) we have about them.
- Premise 2: The opinions we form about people are influenced by what other people think — these people may reinforce or refute the stereotypes.
- Premise 3: Based on what we believe and what we have learned from others, we form our opinions of a group of people (i.e. librarians). Unless something completely disrupts our assumptions, we will continue to believe them.

Looking specifically at the librarian stereotypes:

- Premise 1: We think librarians are old female prudes who only work with books.
- Premise 2: Movies show them as old and young, but all are prudish (or at least sexually repressed) females and they all work with books.
- Premise 3: We decide librarians can be old or young females but they are all a bit prudish and/or repressed and all they do is work with books. These assumptions will hold true until we see a young, stylish, librarian who exemplifies culture's ideals of "sexy" and she's toting a computer or we see a male librarian either with or without technology.

Mead added to Blumer's social interactionism with his idea of the looking glass self. Mead says we socially construct ourselves based on society's — essentially, language's — influence. Our society is our cultural context. We "take the role of the other," we imagine how we look to others, and from this we construct ourselves. "Symbolic interactionists are convinced that the self is a function of language. Without talk there would be no self-concept, so one has to be a member of a community before consciousness of self sets in" (Griffin, 2006, p. 59). This meshes with the existence of stereotypes. Pagowsky and DeFrain (2014) state, "Although stereotypes are literally about us, stereotype existence is about the other: the one who is doing the perceiving" ("But Stereotype Exhaustion," para. 3). After all, stereotypes exist because of what "the other" thinks about us. If we did not have "the other's" opinions to consider, stereotypes wouldn't exist in our minds. The idea of the looking glass self and the concept of "the other" will come up throughout the book because it represents the struggle to be an individual while still conforming enough to expectations to be accepted by society. This socially constructed self leads the author to question whether a profession attracts a stereotypical person or the stereotypes associated with the profession shape the person once the person has entered the profession.

Also, "according to Mead, the self is an ongoing process of combining the 'I' and the 'me.' The 'I' is the spontaneous, driving force that fosters all that is novel, unpredictable, and unorganized in the self…The 'me' is viewed as an object — the image of self seen in the looking-glass of other people's reactions" (Griffin, 2006, p. 60). Thus we are engaged in a constant struggle between our individual selves — "I" — and our socially constructed selves — "me." The "I" may want to break stereotypes while the "me" may be more inclined to adhere to them.

The "me" may not always be socially constructed via direct interactions with others. Mead and other symbolic interactionists refer to the idea of a "generalized other." This "generalized other is an organized set of information that the individual carries in his or her head about what the general expectations and attitudes of the social group are. We refer to this generalized other whenever we try to figure out how to behave or how to evaluate our behavior in a social situation. We take the position of the generalized other and assign meaning to our actions" (Griffin, 2006, p. 61). Griffin adds, "It is unclear whether Mead regarded the generalized other as (1) an overarching looking-glass self that we put together from the reflections we see in everyone we know or (2) the expectations of society that influence every conversation that takes place in people's minds" (p. 61). But is it actually possible to separate these two possibilities? The author does not believe it is possible because society's expectations are molding all of us from the time we are in the womb. These expectations are reflected in people, and that's what we see. Also, the visual media is so omnipresent, bombarding us with the popular ideals in society, that even if we surround ourselves with people who deny society's expectations we are still inundated with reminders of these expectations. Whether we look at a billboard ad, pick up a gender-specific magazine, or watch television, we are subconsciously absorbing messages about society's ideals. The looking-glass self is a perpetual, subconscious reflection of everything we absorb from the environment around us. But the danger of this is stereotype perpetuation simply because stereotypes all become a self-fulfilling prophecy.

Having an "other" helps to create an "us versus them" mentality. Unfortunately we are practically forced into this mentality by the very nature of existence and being born into a culture: "Human infants become adults in a particular human society. Thus, the infant grows into a child and later into an adult not simply as a human but as a particular kind of human: a Kwakiutl, Tobriand, Islander, Buton, or Tahitian" (Nanda & Warms, 2009, p. 25). Hornsey (2008) says Henri Tajfel "argued that the mere process of making salient 'us and them' distinctions changes the way people see each other. When category distinctions are salient, people perceptually enhance similarities within the group ('we're all much the same') and enhance differences among the groups ('we're different from them')" (p. 206). Stereotypes help create this "us" (the "ingroup") versus "them" (the "outgroup") mentality; in fact librarianship has "we" librarians and "those" patrons as well as "we" librarians who break the stereotypes and "those" librarians who perpetuate the stereotype. Unfortunately our profession's internal divisions help to perpetuate stereotypes while we are also fighting them. Hornsey (2008) draws on Festinger to tell us "people evaluate their group with reference to relevant outgroups. Groups are not islands; they become psychologically real only when defined in comparison to other groups" (p. 207). We assign different meaning to the same actions depending on the group performing the actions and the cultural expectations we have for these groups; these meanings may stem from stereotypes. "Thus, the long hours worked by a person associated with an ingroup illustrate his or her devotion, while the same number of hours worked by a person belonging to an outgroup reveals his or her compulsiveness and inability to relax" (Sandstrom, Martin, & Fine, 2010, p. 67). The assignment of different meanings to the same actions is also evident in gender expectations. Men who marry older in life or who do not marry at all are considered bachelors while women who do this are considered old maids. Also, men who have numerous sexual partners are viewed as studs sewing their wild oats while women who do this are viewed as sluts. It follows that "social identity theorists argue that stereotypes have a social function, in the sense that they help legitimize the past and current actions of the ingroup" (Hornsey, 2008, p. 209).

The field of cultural studies extends the idea of your community, or your group, influencing meaning. In Hall's book *Representation*, he states, "The primary function of discourse is to make meaning" because symbols have no inherent meaning. He describes a "give and take of meaning" between individuals and the group as a whole. "To say that two people belong to the same culture is to say that they interpret the world in roughly the same ways and can express themselves, their thoughts, and feelings about the world in ways that will be understood by each other" (as cited in Griffin, 2006, p. 374).

Hall was influenced by Foucault who also believed that signs and symbols cannot be interpreted apart from culture and media messages. According to Foucault, signs and symbols "both require frameworks of interpretation in order to make sense" (as cited in Griffin, 2006, p. 373).

Foucault believed that framework came from the dominant discourse; those in charge in society, the "dominant" group, shape the discourse and by extension the ideas of the day. In terms of librarian stereotypes, we are viewed from the dominant discourse of men; thus we are objectified by the "male gaze" in cinema, and society continues to objectify us and to place less value on "women's work" as has traditionally been the case throughout history. In fact in cinema, librarians in movies aren't just the object of the metaphorical male gaze of the camera, but they are often the objects of the actual gazes of the male characters. Clearly something as simple as a camera angle encourages objectifying female librarians. It is possible, though, to work against the dominant discourse. The idea of working against a dominant discourse gives rise to standpoint theory in communication and gender studies as well as in various forms of literary criticism that encourage us to look at a situation from a different point of view; this is typically the point of view of "the other," of the non-dominant discourse, and we often gain a different understanding of the situation from doing this. For example, a feminist critique would ask us to examine how we would feel about a movie scene if we were looking at it through the eyes of the objectified librarian character rather than through the eyes of the male character objectifying her or through the lens of what society tells her she should be.

Foucault utilized the concept of standpoint theory in a slightly different way. He noted in his work *The History of Sexuality* that when the dominant discourse created the term "homosexuality" for a deviant group, it also created the possibility of a reverse discourse: "homosexuality began to speak on its own behalf, to demand that its legitimacy or 'naturality' be acknowledged, often in the same vocabulary, using the same categories by which it was medically classified" (Culler, 1997, p. 116). When we take a word that signifies oppression and turn it into something that empowers us, we are changing the sign and symbol system and engaging in reverse discourse. Women have done this by embracing the term "bitch," and gays and lesbians have done this by embracing the word "queer." In fact in 1976, Foucault said people have always engaged in what we now view as homosexual practices, but "those practices did not generate or represent an identity until a medicalizing discourse obsessed with repressing sexuality arose in the nineteenth century" (Parker, 2011, p. 189). Parker (2011) adds "the very term *homosexual* did not appear until 1869. In the late nineteenth century, it came into prominence as a diagnosis for what many doctors then considered a sickness." Also, "the word *heterosexuality* did not appear until 1880" (p. 191-192). The term "queer" eventually came to be an insult associated with the "sickness" of homosexuality. Queer Theory takes the name of an insult and makes it a statement of empowerment, turning it into a concept that forces us to acknowledge homosexuality and to see the world through from the standpoint of homosexuals. Weaver (2010a, 2010b) cites examples of racist comedy, where Asians and African Americans actively incorporate racist stereotypes and language into their acts and use humor as a way to challenge and mock dominant discourse. Attebury (2010) examines YouTube videos by and about librarians in which parody is used to challenge the aforementioned stereotypes originated by Seale (2008). When librarians use stereotypes in parody, they are engaging in reverse discourse to highlight the ridiculousness of stereotypes; however, in this case, librarians are using visual and verbal cues to challenge the spinster librarian, sexy librarian, sexually repressed librarian, etc. These visual cues include glasses, buns, sweaters, and book carts.

Foucault's ideas of a dominant and a reverse discourse mesh well with librarianship. Radford and Radford (1997) cite an observation by Irene Diamond and Lee Quimby: "Both [feminism and Foucault] bring to the fore the crucial role of discourse in its capacity to produce and sustain hegemonic power and emphasize the challenges contained within marginalized and/or unrecognized discourses" (p. 252). Radford and Radford believe the female librarian is an example of this convergence. They tell us that the stereotype meshes with the library as a cultural institution, and both represent order and fixed places in their worlds. Librarians are tasked with maintaining order and guarding knowledge; thus libraries and librarians exemplify knowledge and power, yet female librarians are stereotypically represented as women whom no woman aspires to be rather than being represented as powerful, respected individuals. Radford and Radford go on to explain that Foucault sees the library as managing the fears of uncontrolled discourse. "The stereotype of the female librarian can be thought of as a strategy in which this fundamental fear can be managed, defused, and disguised. The female librarian is presented as fearsome, but, beneath the stern exterior, there is nothing to fear: there is only a woman…The power of the librarian is the power of the woman: it is recognized as present, but is afforded little respect…Indeed, the relationship between rationality and the librarian is reversed in the female stereotype: it is the rationality that controls the librarian" (p. 261).

This idea of the rationality controlling the librarian harkens back to the Sapir-Whorf hypothesis in which language shapes our ideas. It is also interesting to see women in the gatekeeper of order role when traditionally men represented rationality and order and women were the irrational others. However the profession began as a man's job because men were traditionally the ones who worked outside of the home. It didn't become a woman's profession until Melville Dewey hired women for cheap labor. We still see men in libraries, but in the higher paid administration roles in which they have power over the (mostly female) librarians. But what Radford and Radford suggest is that the order takes control of the woman and makes her become a spinster slave to her profession; if a woman wants to marry, she must be sure she leaves her profession rather than become a slave to it. Thus dominant discourse is a way of maintaining power, and this can include perpetuating stereotypes if those are the beliefs of the group in power. Reverse discourse can be used to subvert and challenge the dominant discourse to show how stereotypes are wrong.

Gender and its Impact on Work and Professionalism

Gender is "the way society creates, patterns, and rewards our understandings of femininity and masculinity or the process by which roles and appropriate behavior are ascribed to women and men. Gender, in other words, can be understood as the social organization of sexual differences" (Shaw & Lee, 2007, p. 124). "Social" means it happens in the context of society, and our society provides our cultural context. Recall how different cultures view gender differently: "A gender stereotype consists of beliefs about the psychological traits and characteristics of, as well as the activities appropriate to, men or women. Gender roles are defined by behaviors, but gender stereotypes are beliefs about masculinity and femininity" (Brannon, 2005, p. 161). These stereotypical beliefs become the "norms" we associate with each gender. According to Shaw and Lee (2007), "Gender norms provide the standards or parameters through which thoughts and behaviors are molded" (p. 127). It is important to note that gender is not the same as biological sex despite the fact that those terms are often used interchangeably. Gender is a construction that can be independent from your biological sex. Some cultures link these two concepts, and they believe biological sex dictates gender. This is the case in the United States, and thus the terms sex and gender are often used interchangeably in this culture's communication.

Gender differences linked to biological sex are ingrained in our culture, and we see them being ingrained in us even before we are born. For example, finding out the sex of a baby leads to buying specific color clothing and toys. As children grow, we may even teach them different things depending on gender norms; for example, mothers may want to do "girly" things with daughters such as cooking and shopping while fathers want to do "manly" things with sons like sports. Although today's world is seeing gender role lines blurring, particularly when it comes to parenting and domestic chores and responsibilities, the stereotypical male/female gender roles are still perpetuated. Brannon (2005) says, "Women and men are born with biological differences that dictate the basis for different traits and behaviors. Indeed, they are so different that women are the 'opposite sex,' suggesting that whatever men are, women are at the opposite end of the spectrum (p. 2). This terminology itself leads us to believe we are in no way similar; we are each other's "other." While the concept of "the other" has been discussed thus far in relation to symbolic interactionism, the term "other" or "othering" was first used in existential philosophy by Jean Paul Sartre to indicate the negative relation between individuals in which on has selfhood and views another as 'other,' different, and not-self." Simone de Beauvoir expanded on this concept in her 1952 *The Second Sex*. "She argues that in all situations, perspectives and experiences woman is Othered because man sets himself as the norm and with selfhood while the women is constructed as deviant and Other and exists only in relation to man, thus without selfhood" (McHugh, 2007,

p. 90). If we always see each other as opposites where one of the pair is subordinate to the other, if this is the only way of expression our language gives us, are we able to picture ourselves in other ways? If we want our behavior, ideas, abilities, and looks to be able to span the gender spectrum and be completely equal, is that possible with our current cultural ideals and the resulting language?

Gender norms continue to be reinforced throughout our lifetime. As we grow up, Bem (1981) says we develop gender schema. A schema is "a cognitive structure, a network of associations that organizes and guides an individual's perceptions" (as cited in Brannon, 2005, p. 125). "Gender schema theory hypothesizes that children develop gender-related behaviors because they develop schemata that guide them to adopt such behaviors. In this view, gender-related behaviors appear not only as a result of cognitive development, but also because children develop special schemata related to gender. According to gender schema theory, the culture also plays a role in gender development, providing the reference for the formation of gender schemata. Not only are children ready to encode and organize information about gender, but they also do so in a social environment that defines maleness and femaleness" (Bem, 1985, as cited in Brannon, 2005, p. 125). Social learning theory tells us children learn gendered behavior — they develop their gender schema — by observation and imitation and by the rewards and punishments that follow the imitation (Myers, 2005, p. 95). For example, boys are encouraged to imitate their fathers and are discouraged from imitating their mothers. Boys are also discouraged from playing with dolls that are not labeled "action figures." While girls are not specifically told they can't play with toys that boys traditionally play with, such as trucks and tools, this is not exactly encouraged either; this shows that our society thinks it is okay to act like or be a man but it is not okay to act like or be a woman. When toys like this are designed for girls, they come in traditional girl colors such as pink or purple thus drawing attention away from the purpose of the items and back to gender to remind girls they are first and foremost girls. Girls are frequently encouraged to help their mothers take care of the house and take care of others through cooking, cleaning, etc. rather than to help their fathers fix things around the house. Also, it seems the default method of grouping school students together is according to biological sex. "Although parents, teachers, and other school officials often encourage this separation, boys and girls themselves contribute to it…Because they learn and abide by different standards, boys and girls often view themselves and their actions differently. They discover that they…must orient their talk, actions, and selves to one of two gender audiences. Thorne examined this and noted "preadolescent boys and girls regularly cross the gender divide and engage in some group activities, such as kickball and dodgeball, which have a balanced mix. The contacts between genders, however, have a 'with-then-apart' quality, and the 'with' phase is as essential to the maintenance of gender boundaries as the 'apart' phase. During their interactions together, boys and girls often emphasize and display alleged differences, thereby placing themselves on 'opposite sides' and heightening gender boundaries" (Sandstrom, Martin, & Fine, 2010, p. 94-95). The "with-then-apart" concept is illustrated when children play games together but are arranged in "boys versus girls" teams. They are engaging in the same activity, but attributing being a boy or being a girl to doing the activity differently and ultimately to success or defeat. Thus culture helps shape gender views of children by instilling gender norms in their brains from birth; this encourages children to adopt rigid gender roles. Subconsciously adopting gender roles instilled in us since birth makes it that much more difficult to change stereotypes.

Brannon (2005) adds "gender schema theory also predicts that developing gender schema increases accuracy and memory for gender-consistent information compared to gender-inconsistent information;" also, "children tend to change their memories to fit gender-typical activities, such as remembering a man driving a truck when he was pictured cooking. This tendency to distort memory in ways consistent with gender schemata suggests that the development of gender schemata influences the way people interpret information" (p. 126). According to this theory, children are more likely to remember images that confirm gender stereotypes. Thus a child can see a male and a female librarian, but that child is more likely to remember the female librarian because librarians are stereotypically female. Memory studies in the field of psychology help explain why we may remember things in this way. "Michael Ross and his colleagues (1981) found that people unknowingly revise their own histories. After Ross persuaded a group of people that brushing their teeth frequently is desirable, they (more than other people) recalled having brushed their teeth in the last two weeks…To remember our past is often to revise it (Myers, 2005, p. 36). Myers (2005) also tells us "we often construct our memories as we encode them, and we may also alter our memories as we withdraw them from our memory bank." Part of this alteration may be due to the misinformation effect which says "after exposure to subtle misinformation, many people misremember" (p. 308). Misinformation is also a problem when we recount a memory but need to fill in memory gaps. Myers (2005) says we "fill in memory gaps with plausible guesses and assumptions" (p. 308). Constant exposure to stereotypes makes these images seem plausible. Thus if children are constantly exposed to stereotypes that provide misinformation about the profession combined with a tendency to remember in terms of gender schema, our own memory will perpetuate stereotypes. This tendency to think in terms of gender schema also contributes to the perpetuation of stereotypes in the media — the stereotypes are easily identifiable so people can get the gist of your message quickly and in a way that relates to how they already see the world. This indicates that gender roles are so deeply embedded in culture and in our minds that a major cultural shift may be necessary to overcome librarianship being seen as stereotypically female.

Interestingly, although we think in gendered ways, we allow *ourselves* some latitude with boundaries of stereotypes. This could be one reason why stereotypes do change, but they take so long to change. Brannon (2005) says, "Although people hold stereotypical gender views of men and women, they may make exceptions for themselves, allowing themselves a wider variety of behaviors than the stereotype would permit. By allowing such personal exceptions as routine, people decrease the power of stereotypes to control and restrict their lives" (p. 175). Again we see symbolic interactionism in play here. The "I" may win out over the "me" in the negotiation for the development of self. Unfortunately we are still looking at the rest of society as "the other" and think, "*I* can break the stereotypes, but the *others* cannot."

Some of the qualities associated with the female gender schema are closely associated with librarianship; thus it's possible that librarianship could be the ideal, and by extension the ultimate stereotypical, female profession. Throughout history, until women gained equality (and even still to an extent today), women were encouraged to be quiet and obedient, to support men in their pursuits, and to enjoy quiet activities like reading.

Girls were also encouraged to be proper ladies and wear dresses; it seems like the librarian is the perfect career path for a woman because stereotypical librarians should be quiet, like reading, wear dresses, and support the scholarly research and recreational reading pursuits of others. Society essentially raised women to be seen and not heard and, unless spoken to first or the need to shush a patron arises, librarians are stereotypically seen and not heard, and the stereotypical library itself is an institution in which everyone inside of it should be seen and not heard. Society still tends to relegate women to the position of being "seen," even if she is also heard. In fact society encourages women to always be well-coiffed and prepared to be seen because being seen is just as important as, or even more important than, being heard. The cinematic male gaze — the gaze that looks at women as objects only to be seen — is evident in movies, television, ads, and virtually all media. It has become so pervasive that society now has the male gaze ingrained in it even when the gaze is coming from other women — we are taught to first look at and to judge each other's appearances.

    Gender differences and gender norms carry over into the workforce and impact the types of jobs we assign each gender and the value we assign these jobs. Women have offered a supporting role since the Industrial Revolution when paid work moved outside of the home. Women stayed home, ran the household, and took care of the children — they supported the growth of children and the welfare of husbands — rather than earning money outside of the home. Although this supporting role was essential so men could devote their time to paying jobs, it was devalued because it did not produce any kind of paycheck or tangible gains. In fact a woman's place as managing the household was much like Radford and Radford's (1997) idea that the female librarian is a front and shouldn't be feared because the real power lies with the men controlling her and the library. In the case of women and the household, the housewife took care of everything, and without her work the system that allowed men to work outside the home would have collapsed; however she had no real power — her husband had all of the power — and society and even her own children knew this. In fact we still see a woman's position as an equal head of the household devalued, even if she maintains the household in addition to holding down a job, when we hear the phrase, "Wait 'till your father gets home!," as the final straw when a mother is trying to discipline children who just will not listen to her. She isn't telling them, "You will respect my authority because I am your mother." Instead she is telling them, "You aren't listening to me, but you just wait until your father hears about this because you actually respect his authority."

The library profession has traditionally been a profession that supports others from behind the scenes. Librarianship supports the information needs of others, and it does not produce monetary gains as a profitable business may do. With advances in technology, people wonder why the profession is needed; thus the profession itself is devalued and was and still is a perfect fit for women.

However, the profession was not always a traditional woman's field; despite once being occupied by men, librarian positions were not often afforded respect or even valued. Once women came to dominate the field, the value placed on the profession was almost certain to remain stagnant or even to plummet despite a new emphasis on the importance of research and the research movement after the 1876 founding of Johns Hopkins University. Shaw and Lee's (2007) discussion of clerical work becoming a female profession is an example of how occupational gender segregation impacts the value placed on a profession; this can also apply to librarianship: "It is interesting to look at how the development of certain occupations as female segregated has affected the status and conditions of work. For example, clerical work, although low prestige, was definitely a man's job until the turn of the twentieth century when women quickly became associated with this work. This was due to the following factors: there was a large pool of women with few other opportunities; clerical work's low status made it easier for women to be accepted; typewriter manufacturers began promoting the typewriter as something women used; and the personal service aspect of the work fit gender norms about the feminine aspect of secretarial work. As more women entered the profession, the gap between clerical wages and blue-collar wages generally increased, and the status of the clerical profession fell" (p. 448). Thus gender segregation may not simply leave a position's prestige and wages stagnant — it can negatively impact both.

It's interesting to note that these service positions were already low status before women came on the scene; thus women did not make them low status, but our society tends to view lower paying service jobs as lower status jobs. Since women had no choice but to work for less pay, this made them attractive candidates for these service positions. The low pay likely lowered the status of the female dominated professions, almost ensuring that men stayed away from these professions because they were able to take advantage of higher paying positions. This has caused a vicious cycle of low status, low pay, and continued gender segregation.

Padavic and Reskin (2002) state that this sexual division of labor is "a fundamental feature of work" that is and has always been seen in all societies of the world, although the specific jobs delegated to each sex may differ depending on the time and the society (p. 7). In fact, Padavic and Reskin say "the devaluation of women and their activities is deeply embedded in huge major cultures and religions of the world" (p. 10). Padavic and Reskin use the book of Leviticus, chapter 27 verses 3 through 7, in the Bible as an example: female servants are only ascribed three-fifths of the value of male servants (p. 10).

In today's world where women are encouraged to work, these ideas of gender division of labor should be outdated; unfortunately they are anything but outdated. These ideas — these stereotypes — impact how we associate professions with men and women. "Ideas, although based in the interpretive realm of thought and subjectivity, direct our behavior and constrain the ways in which we see each other and others see us. Ideas also have a political reality because they affect how society works, who gets rewarded, and how things should and should not be. For example, if we believe that women's proper place is in the home, we are not likely to object to the sexist practices of employer discrimination. However, if we believe that women are just as capable as men, we are likely to support policy changes that would make opportunities available to them [women]" (Andersen, 1988, p. 24). Brinkerhoff et al. (2008) expand on this: "Gender is also a social structure…Gender is built into social structure when workplaces don't provide day care; women don't receive equal pay; father's don't receive paternity leave; basketballs, executive chairs, and power drills are sized to fit the average man; and husbands who share equally in the housework are subtly ridiculed by their friends" (p. 203). Thus our ideas, which often stem from stereotypes, impact what professions we associate with each gender and how much we value a position that is primarily associated with a specific gender; this value, or lack thereof, in turn impacts how much prestige we assign a position and, consequently, salary and types of job opportunities available within a profession. For example, in librarianship's early days, why would a position that would be filled by a woman who would leave it as soon as she found a husband need to be valued or paid well?

In addition to the value placed on different genders, the communication styles of genders impact the value placed upon us and the profession. Deborah Tannen's theory of genderlect styles of communication says that men and women communicate for different reasons; men aren't necessarily communicating in ways to purposely dominate women and remain the dominant gender. According to Tannen, women communicate more from a desire to connect whereas men communicate out of a desire for status (Griffin, 2006, p. 33). Perhaps this is one reason why we see more men in leadership positions, including library leadership, than women. Our competitive society places more value on talk for status, essentially talk to dominate, than on talk for connections; thus men are seen as more capable and will receive more promotions. This is why we respect women in power for becoming more like men when they adopt the communication style of men, but men's adopting the communication style of women is not valued and then men are often mocked and assumed to be gay. This could also be another reason librarianship remains primarily a female profession both in numbers and in stereotype. A librarian must talk to form connections with patrons rather than talk to show dominance over patrons. Talking to show dominance can lead to patrons seeing the librarian as the policeman or the know it all. Librarians don't want to be seen as imposing figures that are unapproachable, so even our non-verbal communication should encourage connections. Of course either gender is capable of communicating for status or for connections; however if we continue to be predisposed to traditional gender stereotypes, then women will be encouraged to adopt a less domineering communication style than men, and people may find women more approachable because they expect that communication style from them whereas they expect men to be less caring and more authoritative and intimidating. In a society that values competition, communication for connections rather than status may very well shape the abilities women and men have to enter and excel in certain professions.

Underlying history's views on the equality of women and these gender norms is the "nature versus nurture" debate —— does our biology (nature) shape us, or does society shape us into the people we become (nurture)? While nature plays a part in our physical development, including the development of the biological differences we attribute to different genders, it is clear from the theories presented thus far that our culture, the "nurture" side of the debate, predominantly shapes gender while "nature" shapes biology. Historically biology, because biology has been so tied to gender, has been used to ascribe gender differences that were seen as "natural" extensions of our biology. When Harvard, William & Mary, and Yale opened in the 1600s as the first U.S. colleges, "they were only for men. The first governor of Massachusetts [John Winthrop] is often quoted on his diagnosis of the madness of a woman. It was caused, he said, by reading and writing books and doing other unwomanly things…He was only formulating what most people seemed to think: that 'learning' was beyond the capacity of women's brains" (Scott, 1986, p. 401). The Victorian "sex in brain" debate continued this thinking: the "sex in brain" debate is "a long-running debate about the education of women, which was firmly embedded within Darwinistic and anthropological scientific rhetoric. The object in question was to establish the mental differences between men and women; to define them according to natural law; thereby to decide social policy — particularly with regard to education — according to nature" (Boddice, 2011, p. 321). In fact George

Romanes was a pioneer of comparative psychology and a Darwinist who believed "if evolution could be demonstrated through physical difference, it ought also to be demonstrable through mental difference," and he said the fact that women have an average brain weight smaller than men was an indication of their lesser intelligence. This smaller brain weight also meant women's mental ability could not be devoted to both education and childbearing, and an education could actually harm a woman's physical ability to have a child. It also leant itself to the idea that a woman's mind was subject to hysteria, overwhelming emotions, and "comparative childishness" (Boddice, 2011, pp. 324 – 333). These thoughts about women's mental capacity and inclination toward hysteria (they were the "irrational others" to the "rational" men) impacted medical treatment. Parry (2010) tells us, "In the 19th century women were thought to be intrinsically mad by virtue of their femaleness, which made them vulnerable, and women outnumbered men in Victorian asylums almost two to one" ("Frustration," para. 1).

While modern science tells us women's average smaller brain weight (smaller by mere ounces) does not impact their intelligence or make them irrationally hysterical, remnants of this belief still linger today. For example, many people still believe women are more fit to care for children than men are; this is evident in custody cases and even in television commercials that show men as inept fathers if they are depicted as fathers at all. It is also evident when people — and even the media — question a woman's ability to be president of the United States because women are generally soft-hearted and have extreme emotional mood swings when it's "that time of the month."

Stereotypes do not help shed the remnants of the belief that we are inherently different than men by nature. In fact an examination of how embedded these stereotypes and gender norms are in our culture leads this author to believe we are unfortunately seeing a convergence of nature and nurture. Put in the perspective of librarianship, it's become our nature to see women as naturally quiet and reserved and to thus conflate their gender with stereotypical librarian images, and it's our nature to devalue their work. Surely we don't nurture the old maid stereotype of an introverted spinster, but we nurture the feminine beauty and sexuality found in the sexy librarian stereotype and the male authority found in the policeman stereotype. Stereotypes are also nurtured when we allow children to learn and believe them, when the media constantly bombards us with them, and when people don't have a clear enough idea of librarianship to mentally combat the stereotypes. Hence stereotypes are nurturing our nature.

This history of devaluing women's work leads this book's author to question whether or not the stereotypes associated with librarians really matter as long as the field is still ultimately associated with women — we can been seen as old maids, sexy librarians, or powerful guardians of knowledge — but in the end we are "just a female profession" and thus we are devalued. If this is the case, then any attempts to change the stereotype will most certainly require a major cultural shift. This doesn't mean that adopting specific stereotypes won't lead to even more devaluing of the profession; it's possible that embracing a stereotype that enhances femininity (i.e. the sexy librarian) could hurt the profession even more because it is drawing more attention to the idea of this being a female profession.

Media

The media — all forms, such as TV, ads, radio, magazines, books, movies, social media, etc. — reflect society's ideals and have a profound influence on us. "We assume that a wide variety of media messages can act as teachers of values, ideologies, and beliefs and that they can provide images for interpreting the world whether or not the designers are conscious of their intent. An advertisement, for example, may be intended merely to sell cigarettes to women, but incidentally it may encode a message about gender relations and what it means to be a 'woman'" (Gamson, 1992, p. 374). Nealon and Giroux (2004) add to this idea: "Media tell us how to be subjects, or how to be certain types of subjects" (p. 68). Their comments remind us media teach us more than how to be a certain gender, but also how to be a certain age, occupation, etc. Media impact what we think the world is like and what we see as the norm in situations; thus the way genders and/or professions are consistently portrayed can color our opinions of them. "Media portrayals can be so powerful and persuasive that these portrayals become the standard on which people judge what is normal and desirable in their own lives" (Brannon, 2005, pp. 147-148). However Andersen (1988) cites the reflection hypothesis to tell us it works the other way around: reflection hypothesis "assumes that the mass media reflect the values of the general population…although the media images are make-believe, they do symbolize dominant social beliefs and images" (p. 30). Andersen points out the vicious cycle by adding, "Women's depictions in the media can be seen as social myths by which the meaning of society and women's place within it are established…The media establish popular cultures, which in turn establishes our definitions of social reality" (p. 34). These definitions of social reality include gender norms and may very well end up being stereotypes. Thus we are caught in a cycle that further ingrains gender norms and stereotypes into our culture, making them much harder to break. One such norm that's become ingrained in our culture is the ever-increasing objectification and sexualization of people, particularly of women.

It's clear that our society has become increasingly sexualized. Simply comparing ads, movies, and television shows of today to those from 50 years ago shows that skimpier clothing, sexual innuendos and situations, and foul language have become staples of all media genres. "Sex sells" is no longer a novel idea — it's the norm we all abide by. In fact Grabe and Samson (2011) show us an example of this with female news anchors. According to Grabe and Samson, recent lawsuits suggest that broadcast news networks favor younger women as opposed to older (mid-thirties and above) women because of their "audience drawing potential." Also, anecdotal evidence shows the trend of female anchors dressing conservatively has given way to "bold make-up," large jewelry, and often plunging necklines (p. 471-472). With sexual objectification extending beyond entertainment into the realm of news, why would we think librarianship, a predominantly female profession, could escape objectification and sexualization?

Advertising, which invades nearly every aspect of our lives, also invokes and perpetuates stereotypes. In 2007, a *New York Times* article stated, "Consumers' viewing and reading habits are so scattershot now that many advertisers say the best way to reach time-pressed consumers is to try to catch their eye at literally every turn" (Story, 2007, para. 3). Story adds, "Yankelovich, a market research firm, estimates that a person living in a city 30 years ago saw up to 2,000 ad messages a day, compared with up to 5,000 today" (para. 8). This was true in 2007, and it's even more true now. Ads are becoming more invasive, especially when we opt to use free apps and other services. Just how much of these ads and how much of the multiple media feeds someone is watching at any given moment is a debate for another study; however, in a world where we are bombarded with media (we've gone from the "information age" to the "information overload age"), the media messages must be short and easy to grasp. "Advertising has to communicate quickly, using symbols that are easily understandable by a broad audience. Traditional librarian imagery readily fits this bill" (Tobias, 2003, p. 14). Thus ads rely on stereotypes, which are symbols understood by a large number of people in a culture. But ads don't just perpetuate stereotypes of librarians and other professionals, they also perpetuate gender stereotypes. Society places a high value on youth and beauty, as was exemplified by Grabe and Samson's (2011) news anchor example, so of course "many ads seemed designed to make women fearful — fearful of aging, fearful of being overweight, fearful of being alone" (Andersen, 1988, p. 23). Ads are perpetuating feminine ideals and stereotypes via fear, which is an extremely powerful emotion whose effects are difficult to reverse. Interestingly the characteristics ads are designed to make women fear are all embodied in the old maid librarian stereotype — old age, loss of beauty, and spinsterhood.

Attebury (2010) adds stereotypes alleviate information overload because "putting items into categories saves energy by requiring a person to understand only one category rather than each of the individual items in it" (p. 1). This is why TV shows and movies often have stock characters that display the stereotypical qualities of a certain group — viewers don't have to think hard (or sometimes at all) and they can easily understand what's happening even if they aren't fully engaged with what they are watching. We engage less as we multitask more, so it's likely media will continue to use stereotypical stock characters.

But even if those of us with heavy media viewing habits only passively engage with the programs, we are still subconsciously absorbing these stereotypical stock images. Gerbner's cultivation theory, though originally developed to explain how violence on TV impacts people's views of real-life violence, can be applied to saturation of consistent images of any kind via any media outlet. According to Gerbner, "At its root, television is society's institutional storyteller…Television dominates the environment of symbols" (Griffin, 2006, p. 385). In Gerbner's studies, TV violence led heavy TV viewers to believe certain aspects of society related to violence and the police; their beliefs reflected TV's influence. Gerbner says this attitude impact happens as a result of years of build up. Gerbner uses the term "mainstreaming" to "describe the process of 'blurring, blending, and bending' that those with heavy viewing habits undergo. He thinks that through constant exposure to the same images and labels, television types develop a commonality of outlook that doesn't happen with radio." This happens with TV because the attempt of TV is to broadcast, or attract a large number of people, while radio narrowcasts, or heavily segments, its audience (Griffin, 2006, p. 389-390). Narrowcasting means radio doesn't have to rely on stock characters to easily and quickly appeal to everyone who could possibly be listening. "Mainstreaming" is not exclusive to television violence, though. Landridge, Riggi, and Schultz (2014) discuss L.J. Shrum's findings related to television and memory: "Television viewing affects the construction of real-world judgments through its effects on the accessibility of information from memory. Heavy viewers are able to easily recall these familiar media constructs as a basis for their judgments based on the frequency, recency, and vividness of the stereotype. These findings suggest that television viewing supports typical archetypes rather than changing attitudes, which is consistent with Gerbner's view of long-term television effects" ("Perceived Approachability of Librarians," para. 2). These archetypes — or stereotypes — "tend to be very traditional. In fact, the assumed differences between the genders very often drive the plot of television programming" (Shaw and Lee, 2007, p. 505). Gerbner's and Shrum's findings are supported by psychology's concept of heuristics. Myers (2005) says heuristics are mental shortcuts we use to help us make snap decisions. The representativeness heuristic is used to "judge the likelihood of things in terms of how well they represent particular" groups in your mind (p. 321). For example, if someone says, "Dr. Smith is an excellent surgeon," we are likely to assume Dr. Smith is a man because men are often associated with being doctors, particularly surgeons, while women are often associated with being nurses. "The availability heuristic operates when we base our judgments on the availability of information in our memories. If instances of an event are easily available — if they come to mind readily — we presume such events are common (Myers, 2005, p. 322). This means the more often we see something, the more likely we are to believe it is true; thus heavy television viewers who only ever see stereotypical depictions of certain groups, such as librarians, will be more likely to believe those stereotypes are true based on the way our memory functions. Clearly librarian stereotypes can easily become mainstreamed into our consciousness along with the gender and linguistic ideals that help to perpetuate the stereotypes.

Movies are no better when it comes to displaying stereotypical characters. Williamson (2002) did a study applying the Myers-Briggs personality test to movie depictions of librarians to determine what personality traits and personality characteristics they were pictured as having: "The results reveal that filmmakers reinforce positive and negative stereotypes and sex roles in their depictions of librarians' personality types…with librarians, the characteristics often include helpfulness, idealism, or a tendency to enforce the rules, as well as certain gender stereotypes" (pp. 55-56).

But in addition to invoking stereotypes via the use of stock characters, movies reinforce gender stereotypes and the objectification of women via the lens of the camera and the way it looks at women. "One of the first to address the complex question of looking and its relation to gender, John Berger argued that patriarchal society constructed women as an object for the male spectator…Berger maintained that looking is not a neutral activity but carries with it relations of power, access, and control" (Adams, 2000, p. 290-291). In terms of film, Laura Mulvey calls the looking done by the camera the "male gaze." According to Shaw and Lee (2007), "Mulvey argues that movies are essentially made through and for the male gaze to fulfill a voyeuristic desire for men to look at women as objects. Viewers are encouraged to 'see' the movie through the eyes of the male protagonist who carries the plot forward" (p. 506). Parker (2011) tells readers "this male gaze" of the camera that is accomplished through both filming and editing is sometimes referred to as "the masculinization of spectators, because through gendering the camera and the editing, the conventions of film can sway spectators — women and men both — into identifying with a masculine subject position (stance or point of view)" (p. 67). Shaw and Lee (2007) tell us "some feminist scholars have suggested the possibility for 'subversive gazing' by viewers who refuse to gaze the way filmmakers expect and by making different kinds of movies" (p. 506). "Subversive gazing" invokes the concept of Wood's standpoint theory, which encourages us to look at a text or a scenario from various points of view, particularly from the points of view of marginalized groups. For example, would movie scenes look any different from the point of view of the librarian? How do things change when we are seeing them through the eyes of the objectified rather than those of the objectifier?

Media can play a role in perpetuating or defying stereotypes even when that is not the intent. For example, Jesella (2007) published a *New York Times* article about librarians entitled A Hipper Crowd of Shushers; while the headline tells us we are hipper, it also implies we are still nothing more than "shushers." Jesella goes on to explain an evening at a bar with a gathering of people in their 20s and 30s: "With their thrift-store inspired clothes and abundant tattoos, they looked as if they could be filmmakers, Web designers, coffee shop purveyors or artists…The group's members were librarians. Or, in some cases, guybrarians" (paras. 1, 6). Jesella falls back on the stereotype that librarians are typically women by naming male librarians "guybrarians." This may seem harmless, but the need to give men performing traditionally female work a special name is often done as a way to point out how unnatural this behavior is for men; for example, a man who takes care of his children and is called "Mr. Mom" is having his performance of "women's duties" called out and his masculinity called into question whereas calling him a father, which he is, would simply imply he's doing his duty as a parent. Jesella goes on to ask, "How did such a nerdy profession become cool — aside from the fact that a certain amount of nerdiness is now cool?" (para. 27). She has labeled the profession "nerdy" in the sense of that word being an insult. Finally, Jesella tells readers librarianship "is perfect for creative types who want to pursue their passions outside of work and don't want to finance their pursuits by waiting tables" (para. 28). Essentially she is telling people that librarianship is the perfect job for people who would rather be doing something else. Borrelli (2013), in his article about an American Library Association conference in Chicago, also described librarians as hip: "Tina

Louise Happ, an associate librarian at Pritzker Memorial Library in Chicago, wore cool white frame glasses that screamed hipster librarian" (para. 26).

Dilevko and Gottleib (2004) studied how librarians were represented in *New York Times* obituaries from 1977-2002; in their study of 123 obituaries, 78 (63.4%) were men and 45 (36.6%) were women while 50 (40.7%) were affiliated with academic libraries, 34 (27.6%) with special libraries, and 23 (18.7%) with public libraries (pp. 156-157). "Whether by building a collection, overseeing an institution's expansion, sharing expertise through published work, or drawing attention to important issues, librarians acted in a way that provided assistance to library users in the abstract and to scholarship or society as a whole. But only six obituaries described librarians helping individual colleagues and patrons through direct interaction" (pp. 169-170). This depiction shows the profession as exciting, heroic, and predominantly male. It also emphasizes the importance of academic libraries and downplays the importance of public libraries. While this depiction is positive, it is misleading. Daily, mundane tasks are more prevalent and no less important than heroic acts that contribute to scholarship, females dominate the profession, and the work of public libraries and other types of libraries is just as important as the work of academic libraries.

Clearly media images are powerful, but why are they so powerful? According to Brannon (2005), "One reason that media have become so persuasive is the tendency toward what Gregg Easterbrook (1999) called synthesized realism, or a mixture of actual information with phony details blended into a realistic portrayal that is really fiction. When this is done with sufficient skill, people cannot tell the difference" (pp. 147 – 148). This synthesized realism combined with heavy media viewing habits in which the media we view are inundated with stereotypical stock characters creates a perfect cultivation theory storm — we continue to see objectification and sexualization of society, especially of women, as well as traditional gender and professional roles as the norm, as the way society really is or at least the way it should be.

CHAPTER 5

The Sexy Librarian Stereotype and its Impact on the Profession

When Seale (2008) originally created the four librarian stereotype categories, the sexy librarian wasn't there. When Attebury (2010) examined YouTube videos about librarians (made by librarians and non-librarians), she added three additional categories, one of which was the sexy librarian. Rather than just adding the sexy librarian category to the list, Attebury suggests this stereotype is displacing Seale's old maid stereotype. While Attebury's categorizing of the sexy librarian stereotype makes it seem like it was a new stereotype, the truth is this stereotype has been the "other" in the background since the early days of librarian depictions in movies; it is only recently, though, that this stereotype was emphasized and brought to the forefront of our minds. This chapter examines how this stereotype has always been lurking in the background and what the implications of this stereotype are for the profession.

Seale (2008) described the old maid librarian as a repressed, sexless prude; others writing about stereotypes echo this description. Numerous depictions also show the old maid librarian as old, prudish, and single while the young, attractive librarians (yes, there have always been sexy librarians although they were not overtly sexy) leave the profession for marriage; these sexy librarians were always women and were the foil of the old maid. This provided a subliminal message of what women should and should not become, and so the old maid librarian has traditionally represented what women did not want to be — single, unmarried women who had careers and no husbands or families. The sexy librarians were conservatively sexy, which was appropriate for their time periods, but their ambition was not to remain a librarian. The message here was that sexy librarians became wives and mothers, and becoming the old maid librarian was a cautionary tale in a time when a married woman's place was in the home.

The sexy librarian stereotype has always been there, but a cultural shift has allowed it to be the dominant stereotype we are now consciously aware of. Over time, society's values have changed. Women may now have careers, marriages, and families; the career woman is no longer the epitome of what a woman does not want to become. Society has generally accepted that woman can, and often must, have careers outside of the home. Perhaps this is why, as Attebury (2010) says in her evaluation of YouTube videos, "Overall 18% of non-librarian [created] videos analyzed made reference to the sexy librarian while 10% of all non-librarian [created] videos also combined this characteristic with that of the Old Maid. True Old Maid stereotypes are uncommon, suggesting that concerns about spinsterhood are no longer common enough to cause a proliferation of videos based on Donna Reed-like stereotypes" (p. 8).

But this change in attitudes about a woman's ability to have a career coincided with our own desires as librarians to not be associated with the old maid librarian stereotype. The old maid librarian brought with it implications of our approachability as well as our ability to perform 21st century duties, thus we were happy to get away from that and be seen as approachable, friendly, and tech savvy. If approachable meant we had to allow ourselves to be seen as sexy, that was okay; after all, it's no secret that in today's society, sex sells and being sexy is highly valued. People don't aspire to be plain and overlooked, but instead aspire to some level of physical attractiveness. The media constantly perpetuate the idea that no matter what a woman chooses to do in life, she must also — and very often above all else — be beautiful and sexy. Media depictions are powerful, and their omnipresence reinforces stereotypes to allow people to easily determine stock characters, products, etc. "Popular culture forms in particular are very seductive; they reflect and create societal needs, desires, anxieties, and hopes through consumption and participation" (Shaw & Lee, 2007, p. 503). We consume these images and allow ourselves to believe them as long as there is a grain of truth to the depictions. If women are taught that being attractive is something to attain and we strive for that, then of course we will allow ourselves to extend this to the librarian profession and imagine that the prudish, repressed librarian becomes a sexual dynamo when she lets down her hair, takes off her glasses, and unbuttons her blouse. Perhaps this is another reason librarians are willing to be seen as sexy, even via parody, as long as they are not seen as old maids. This desire to be seen as sexy combined with society's acceptance of the need for women to remain in the workforce leads librarians to willingly embrace one stereotype that the media is perpetuating so it displaces another stereotype.

As mentioned earlier, the sexy librarians were in the background of media depictions. These librarians were young, fashionable, conservatively beautiful, sometimes flirtatious, and they were objectified by the cinematic male gaze; however they always left the profession for marriage and families, so they were never defined by their profession and were never consciously thought of as the sexy librarian. They were simply women who worked until it was time to settle down.

While the stereotype wasn't consciously thought about at that time, the male gaze was already starting to objectify and sexualize the profession, thus planting the seeds of the stereotype. This is evident in many library movies, particularly in 1921's *The Lost Romance,* the first movie to show librarians using a ladder and thus the first time a man was able to catch a glimpse of a sexy librarian's ankle while she was on the ladder, leading us all to fantasize about everything else that's forbidden and hidden beneath her skirt. Tevis and Tevis (2005) tell us this movie became "a standard cinematic treatment for two women reel librarians in the same scene — the actress in the leading role is young and attractive, while the second librarian, a supporting actress, is middle-aged and spinsterish in appearance" (p. 9).

From that time forward, the sexy librarian existed in a more overt manner. Attention was specifically drawn to her sexiness or at least to the naughtiness of the mystery of what lies beneath her clothing. Decades later, librarians began embracing and championing sexuality and the sexy librarian. In 1972, Kathleen Glab began encouraging librarians to be more progressive in her chapter in the compendium *Revolting Librarians*. According to Squires (2014), Glab encouraged "librarians to 'practice a few sensuous exercises'...The sensuous librarian, thought Kathleen Glab, would act as an antidote to the common misperception 'that all librarians had silver hair, wore half glasses, tailored suits, sensible shoes, and had their index fingers permanently frozen into a pointing position'" (para. 1). Thus it would seem as if librarians were instrumental in moving the sexy librarian stereotype forward. However, in 1971 — a year before *Revolting Librarians* — a writer under the pseudonym Rod Waleman published *The Young Librarian* which, according to Squires, "marks the emergence of a pornographic subgenre that presents librarians less as old maids and more often as attractive young women, inhibited by library decorum but congenitally oversexed" (para. 1). This placed the emphasis on the library itself as a repressive institution, one that binds women into a prudish life that they want to break free from. Squires goes on to tell us, "The sexy librarian emerges from what Candi Strecker describes as 'the erotic potential of the library setting' with its distinctive mix of public and private space organized by isolated stacks" ("Libraries: Lusty or Musty?," para. 1).

The emergence of library porn coinciding with a call for librarians to be sensuous makes the case for reverse discourse — librarians were now combining the freedom women earned with the sexual revolution with the repressive nature of the old maid stereotype in a way that allowed them to control their sexuality rather than having it be controlled for them. In fact Adams (2000) does not specifically mention becoming a sexy librarian, but does encourage librarians to embrace and play with the old maid stereotype, and this is what we see being done with the sexy librarian stereotype: "Since identity is defined by a logic of exclusion, is it not far better for librarians to play with and subvert the Old Maid stereotype than to have it hum in the background as some repressed yet cacophonously loud other?" (p. 294). Adams's statement also brings to light an important point. She invokes Mead's looking glass self by referring to the old maid stereotype as "the other" — the old maid is not the librarian I am, but is the other, the one I am not. Thus we see this dichotomy which exists within the profession itself — the old maid stereotype is the "other" that no librarian aspires to be.

Proponents of reverse discourse in literary theory warn us that reverse discourse, if not done correctly, can backfire and ultimately serve to further perpetuate the stereotype. The sexy librarian stereotype is an interesting example of this since it grew out of a combination of objectifying librarians and the sexual revolution which allowed women to take control of their sexuality. The sexy librarian stereotype epitomizes the bifurcation of femininity. Shaw and Lee (2007) tell us "a key aspect of femininity is its bifurcation or channeling into two opposite aspects. These aspects involve the chaste, domestic, caring mother or Madonna and the sexy, seducing, fun-loving playmate or whore" (p. 133). Clearly librarian depictions have represented this bifurcation. While at one time these representations appeared in two different women — the sexy librarian who left her career for marriage and the chaste old maid who dedicated her life to the library — we now see it in the same woman. The sexy librarian stereotype often borrows images from the old maid librarian but in a way that makes these images playful and seductive. For example, the sexy librarian has acquired the old maid's bun, glasses, sweater (not a bulky sweater by any means), and skirt (not a skirt that covers her ankles, though). But the sexy librarian displays this imagery in a way that leaves us wanting more, a way that draws us in and makes us want to see what she is hiding. The sexy librarian wants to break free of chastity and/or sexual repression, and she wants to do it in a place that forbids anything "naughty." She is chaste on the outside, but on the inside she is a whore waiting for the right man to help her let down her hair.

Ultimately we are left to wonder if the sexy librarian stereotype is really all that bad. At first is seems that this is a positive stereotype that at least lets people see us as approachable and anything but the prudish old maid whose only desire in life is to "shush" people. Unfortunately, while the sexy librarian may at first appear to be a positive stereotype whose sexuality gives her the confidence and ability to have control over men (this makes it seem like successful reverse discourse because the librarian is using signs of a negative stereotype and turning it into something positive), ultimately in stereotypical depictions she "lets down her hair" for a man's pleasure because she physically desires the man; the man is still in power because his attractiveness is dictating her sexual release.

This is yet another depiction of female objectification as opposed to reverse discourse, and this objectification has consequences.

According to Johnson and Gurung (2011), objectification theory "posits that in western culture, women are targets of the male gaze and socialized into roles that are overly preoccupied with appearances and how others see them" (Frederickson & Roberts 1997, as cited in Johnson & Gurung, p. 178). Johnson and Gurung add that this leads women to internalize this objectification and to "self objectify," or be very critical of their self and their appearance (p. 178). This self-objectification creeps into women's opinions of themselves and their opinions of other women, and it impacts the views we have of each other's competence. In fact a culture of objectifying women has seeped so deep into our collective psyche that Johnson and Gurung tell us, "Overall, when it comes to competence, research has shown that a woman's ability is often assumed to be inferior to that of a man's unless directly proven otherwise." They go on to tell us that ratings of femininity are tied to ratings of objectification and competence in women; they cite research that shows women dressed provocatively are thought to be more feminine than those who are not dressed provocatively, and women who are judged as more competent are often judged as less feminine (p. 179). Thus the sexy librarian's provocative dress will make her seem more feminine; unfortunately, to be judged competent, she should be seen as less feminine. Johnson and Gurung decided to test these notions about femininity, competency, and self-objectification with their own study in which the same woman was depicted performing various tasks while wearing different outfits which varied from more conservative to more provocative. Women then judged the model's levels of competence and femininity. Their study "provided evidence that even when dressed in a provocative manner, if a woman shows competence it will affect both the degree to which other women objectify her as well as the degree to which they perceive her as capable" (p. 184). The researchers did find something different in their research as opposed to others: "In terms of Personal Characteristics, one of the variables that stood out in relation to previous studies was that of the model's perceived femininity. That is, even though previous research has shown that objectified women will be seen as more feminine (Gurung and Chrouser 2007), the study showed that even when provocatively dressed, displaying competence significantly reduced participants' ratings of femininity on the model." From this it could be inferred that just displaying competence overcomes negative connotations of the sexy librarian stereotype. However Johnson and Gurung admit this discrepancy may be due to the fact that the model was seen doing a math problem while provocatively dressed, and since math is inherently seen as a more masculine field this may have clouded the participants' judgment (p. 184). Had the model displayed competence in a field that's not considered inherently masculine, it's possible there may have been different results.

While Johnson and Gurung tell us objectification harms women — and we can extend this to mean it will harm the library profession since the profession is primarily composed of women — Grabe and Samson (2011) explain how studies show that, regardless of gender, people deemed attractive according to cultural values are seen as professionally more competent than those seen as unattractive; this is known as the "what is beautiful is good" hypothesis (p. 475). The "what is beautiful is good" hypothesis should lead us to believe that the sexy librarian stereotype is incredibly beneficial to the profession; however, the stereotype could tip the scales in the opposite direction. Grabe and Samson cite additional studies that show make up enhances femininity but could also be detrimental for women: "It appears that high levels of attractiveness might have detrimental influences on a woman's professional cachet" (p. 476).

The work of Johnson and Gurung along with Grabe and Samson illustrate the double bind that women continue to be in — there's a constant struggle between competence and femininity. It is interesting to note that no similar stereotypes exist for male librarians — there is no male version of the sexy librarian nor is there a male version of the old maid — and men do not face a double bind related to competency versus masculinity. While women have been depicted in relation to their sexuality, men have been depicted in relation to their ability to do the job. Men are either the library policemen who enforce the rules, or they are the inept librarians who really don't do their jobs well; the only stereotypes that address men's sexuality are the underlying stereotype that men in women's work must be gay, but this is not one of the categorized stereotypes in the literature, and the gatekeeper stereotype which encompasses masculinity as well as competence and the need to protect others. Media has often depicted men being inept when it comes to taking on traditional women's roles such as parenting, so it seems fitting that men are depicted as inept at performing the tasks of a traditionally women's profession. Women are traditionally not portrayed as inept librarians; in fact throughout the history of library depictions, the intelligence required for women to be librarians has never been questioned; this intelligence has simply been eclipsed by the social implications of femininity. Unfortunately competence and femininity tend to be inversely related, and we see this struggle in the debate over whether or not the sexy librarian is a positive or a negative stereotype. This struggle exists because the sexy librarian epitomizes the bifurcation of femininity and, rather than that bifurcation coming together to empower women and by extension the profession, it continues to hurt us. After all, if the sexy librarian is the epitome of femininity, that means librarianship has yet another hurdle to jump in order to prove itself as something professional, as something other than just a "female profession."

CHAPTER 6

Public Perceptions of Librarians and Libraries

For almost as long as researchers have been examining stereotypes about librarians, they have also been examining public perceptions of librarians. Media representations impact public perceptions of people and professions, even if those perceptions are subconscious. But overall, have the negative stereotypes been leading to negative public perceptions of librarians? In the literature, there are various responses to this question.

In 2003, Kneale (2009) conducted a "Where's the Librarian" survey and the results were published in her 2009 book *You Don't Look Like a Librarian*. Kneale conducted this survey because, "After finding out what we *perceive* to be patrons' perceptions of librarians, I thought it was time to ask the patrons directly" (p. 157). Her survey was available for a three month period, and it was placed on the main and catalog pages of eight libraries; the libraries were public, academic, and special libraries. She received 782 responses. Kneale did not directly ask patrons about the traits possessed by their librarians, but she did ask the patrons a variety of questions which revealed respondents do ask librarians for help. In fact, more than 90% of the respondents would be comfortable talking to a male librarian, female librarian, older librarian, younger librarian, and a casually dressed librarian. Also, 89.3% would be comfortable talking to a librarian that's conservatively dressed (p. 158 – 165). Kneale went on to ask if people think a college degree is necessary to be a librarian and if the patrons thought anyone who worked in a library was a librarian. Responses to these questions indicate that while people may feel comfortable approaching a librarian (or someone they think is a librarian), the majority of respondents do not understand the education required to become a librarian and they can't distinguish between a librarian and other library employees.

Seale (2008) discussed media stereotypes, most of which were negative, but also cited examples that lead us to believe public perceptions of librarians are generally positive; they are often referred to as "helpful" individuals. However Seale also cites studies that show that the general public doesn't view librarians as professionals and really has no firm understanding of what librarians do and the education that is required for this position. Seale even cites an article by Fagan that shows faculty members and undergraduate students lack an understanding of what their librarians can do to help them, and they also don't understand the skills their librarians possess. A lack of understanding of librarian skills on the part of faculty can be detrimental to a college student's success. Now that libraries are engaging in assessment, more and more research is showing that information literacy skills contribute to college student success, which in turn contributes to retention. In fact the Association of College & Research Libraries' (2015) latest report from its Assessment in Action project sites the following findings: "Library instruction builds students' confidence with the research process. Library instruction contributes to retention and persistence, particularly for students in first-year experience courses and programs. Students who receive library instruction as part of their courses achieve higher grades and demonstrate better information literacy competencies than students who do not receive course-related library instruction…Collaborative instructional activities and services between the library and other campus units (e.g. writing center, study skills, and tutoring services) promote student learning and success" (pp. 1-2).

Also, anecdotally and in surveys related to information literacy, librarians report that faculty buy-in is one of the most important factors in getting students to use the library and to take library instruction seriously.

Majid and Haider (2008) echo Fagan's findings, but Majid and Haider's survey was conducted in Singapore which has been praised for its technological advances in libraries. These authors tell readers that stereotypes are important to understand because they impact who wants to enter the profession (a profession that is not highly regarded will not attract the best and brightest candidates). In addition, Majid and Haider wanted to see if Singapore's technology initiatives have helped to change the stereotypes of librarians. According to these authors, "Libraries in Singapore have invested heavily in constructing modern, highly functional and attractive library buildings as well as developing sophisticated IT infrastructures…Certain creative, innovative, and revolutionary initiatives of these libraries…have been replicated in many parts of the world" (p. 232). Majid and Haider add, "The literature review suggest that despite a paradigm shift in the role and responsibilities of librarians, they still suffer from stereotypes and misperceptions all over the world. Libraries in Singapore, particularly public and academic libraries, are considered very sophisticated, modern, stylish and well stocked." Unfortunately Majid and Haider's survey reveals that while their libraries may be cutting edge in terms of technology and collections, the content doesn't change views of the librarians themselves. Patrons in this study chose the personality traits they associated with librarians, and the top five in order were: helpful, bookish, friendly, orderly, and boring (p. 238). Although patrons recognized librarians' helpfulness, they again failed to realize the professional nature of a librarian's job and the tasks they complete.

Poulin (2008) took a different direction in studying librarian depictions to determine whether public perceptions of librarians are generally positive or negative. Rather than looking at television and film depictions of librarians, Poulin studied YouTube videos created by both librarians and non-librarians. This study gives valuable insight into how patrons see us because the YouTube videos are created by the public itself as opposed to being a media depiction created for public consumption. According to Poulin, "Recent literature seems to indicate there is an increasingly higher percentage of positive images of librarianship in television and film" (p. 2). Poulin cites the emergence of the American Library Association's 2007 documentary *The Hollywood Librarian* as a positive but inherently biased depiction of librarians. He goes on to discuss studies that tell us that the images of old maid librarians, which were always a negative view of librarians, have been decreasing and even disappearing. In addition to the old maid disappearing, Poulin tells us that images such as Noah Wyle's portrayal of librarian Flynn Carson in *The Librarian* and the character of Rupert Giles, high school librarian and slayer watcher in *Buffy the Vampire Slayer,* have generally been received as positive depictions. Poulin adds, "It is noteworthy to point out that these two depictions often cited as being the two most positive portrayals of librarians in years are both men" (pp. 3-4). What Poulin does not mention, and what the accolades these two depictions receive tend to overlook, is the fact that neither Flynn nor Giles have any actual librarian training. Flynn doesn't even perform library duties; at least Giles represents the help librarians provide in the quest for knowledge. Unfortunately neither representation paints a full picture of the career or of the education required to be a librarian. Ultimately Poulin's analysis concludes that the vast majority of images of librarians in YouTube videos created by non-librarians are negative: "While analysis of traditional electronic mass media could lead us to believe that stereotypes of librarians are being combated and overcome, the argument can now be made that a new batch of equally-unflattering images is currently developing" (p. 7). "The YouTube library seems to be employed predominantly by men — often an obsessive compulsive disorder-filled enforcer who takes his job far too seriously…and who at times can have a rather violent or maniacal streak. The female librarians that are featured are not sexually-repressed middle-aged dowdy women, but are rather highly sexually-charged, and seem to be clearly present only to be objectified to the point where there *[sic]* are occasionally targeted for some extremely degrading actions. And on the whole, the library as a place appears to be a soulless, authoritarian center where the only fun occurs when pranks or inappropriate behavior takes place" (p. 5). Poulin does admit that this research may not be generalizable to the public who is not creating YouTube videos, but because the videos are created by the public they are important to examine.

Attebury (2010) extends Poulin's observations and suggests that librarians might want to embrace parody, as non-librarians have, in creating YouTube videos. Attebury's research confirms Poulin's discovery that the majority of videos about libraries/librarians that are created by non-librarians are negative — 93% of the videos in her survey were found to invoke either individually or in combination the old maid, policeman, and inept librarian stereotypes (p. 6). But she also points out that "a sizeable minority of videos created by non-librarians also fall into the parody category. Given that parody may be a way to sincerely point out flaws with the unsavory stereotypes or at least inspire viewers to reconsider the notion that stereotypes are factual, concrete representations, the fact that more than one in five videos overall have made use of it is encouraging" (p. 6). Attebury suggests more librarians take cues from the public and use parody in their videos (at the time of her study, some librarian-created videos used parody but the majority were the librarian as hero/ine or were simply informational videos about library services). Attebury explains how YouTube allows for culture jamming which "involves challenging the dominant images that mass media throws at society by turning that media on itself and parodying the images presented in order to alter their message" (p. 4), and essentially suggests librarians engage in culture jamming when she suggests they engage in parody. Attebury is basically suggesting librarians engage in reverse discourse to show people how ridiculous stereotypes are and to explain to the public what librarians actually do.

In 2013, Landridge, Riggi, and Schultz (2014) conducted a survey at Niagara University to determine whether or not media stereotypes impacted students' perceptions of librarians. Only 360 out of 2,900 students completed the survey and, out of those 360, only 199 completed the survey in its entirety, but the results can be seen as promising. According to the researchers, "Our results indicate that there is not a direct link between exposure amount and particular media content and student judgments of librarian usefulness" ("Student Results," para. 2). Unfortunately comments revealed some conflicting and troubling points. Students said librarian wardrobes didn't impact their opinions of librarian approachability, but students then said they thought their own wardrobes were an important part of presenting themselves to the public; clearly they do believe wardrobe is important ("Student Results," para. 6). Also, when students had a choice, most chose to approach female rather than male librarians ("Student Results," para. 9). Despite the desire to approach female librarians when possible, the researchers also discovered gender bias due to stereotypes about abilities: "It was surprising to find that a few females made comments that suggested that they do not think their gender knows as much as males in certain areas of academia," such as statistics ("Student Results," paras. 10-11). Here we see females undermining their own gender's intelligence based on gender stereotypes that are often omnipresent since birth. It's possible we also see the effects of self-objectifying and being critical of abilities. The researchers concluded that a student's experience with a librarian is more powerful than media representations, but added, "If an individual interacts with a person demonstrating stereotypical behavior…that stereotype will influence all other interactions that individual has with any other member of that group" ("Conclusion," para. 1). This is yet another reason it's important for librarians to understand stereotypes and public perceptions; unfortunately it also contributes to divisions within the profession and creating an undesirable "other" out of people who do have stereotypical qualities because that's part of their personality regardless of profession.

In 2014, Pagowsky and DeFrain sought to figure out why academic library instruction is so difficult to get faculty to accept when it's been around since the 1970s; the authors focused on the impressions faculty and students have of librarians as being a contributing factor to this difficulty: "There are a number of dimensions regarding perception that interested us — both being instruction librarians at research universities — and through doing our own research of the educational psychology literature on impression management (this means what it sounds like: managing others' impressions of us), there seemed to be a strong tie-in with perceptions of librarians, i.e. our stereotypes" (para. 4). Pagowsky and DeFrain cited studies that show faculty and students do not understand what librarians do, but they also cited studies that focused on warm versus cold traits and how this impacts views of competence. The authors distilled down the research about warm versus cold and warm versus competent to tell readers that when people are seen as warm (likeable), they may not be seen as competent; when people are seen as cold (not likeable), they may be seen as competent. Librarianship is not automatically awarded the notion of being warm simply because it's a female profession; in fact the old maid stereotype and policeman stereotype present very cold images of librarians. Also, the fact that librarianship is considered a female profession hurts our ability to be seen as both warm and competent — they cite a study by Cuddy, Glick, and Beninger (2011) that says the "mutual exclusivity" of warmth and competence applies to women. Thus women who are seen as warm *are not* seen as competent while men who are seen as warm *can be* seen as competent. This puts the profession in a bind because we are stereotypically viewed as a female profession, which is a strike against us already, and we want to be seen as warm so patrons approach us but at the same time we need to be seen as competent. The authors note that the sexy librarian and, more recently, the hip librarian were used by librarians to reverse previous stereotypes (reverse discourse), but just because these images portray the librarian as anything but cold does not mean they make the librarian look competent. They are "just as detrimental by simply replacing old stereotypes with new ones while still focusing on the inherent femininity of librarianship" (Pagowsky & DeFrain, 2014, "Maybe We Are Cold?," para. 4). The authors tell us that ultimately we must be competent and warm and combine masculine and feminine traits so that the public understands what we have to offer and what it can learn from us.

The literature throughout the decades has been a mixed bag of positive and negative views of librarians. Studies show that the views of librarians are generally positive despite not knowing what it is librarians actually do, while media created by patrons depicts librarians in a negative light. Whether the depictions have been positive or negative, one thing is clear in all of these studies — the public lacks a clear understanding of what it is librarians actually do and what education they need to do it.

Brian Kenney (2013) wrote an article for *Publisher's Weekly* that provided an overview of the profession for prospective librarians. According to Kenney, "Librarianship is a notoriously opaque profession" and most people have no idea what we do (para. 2). Research shows Kenney's observations are correct. Kenney describes the essence of the profession as this: "Librarianship today is about greeting each customer (in person or online) and making sure that his or her library visit is one of the best experiences of the day. Most importantly, it's about listening to our users' needs and connecting them with information, resources, and services that can help them get on with their lives. Librarianship isn't about what we have; it's about what we do" ("You Had Me at 'Hello'," paras. 2-3). Unfortunately as we have seen above, particularly in the Majid and Haider study, librarians and their quest to improve public perception has long focused on what the library has as opposed to what librarians do; this is quite possibly one of the reasons people still have little to no idea what librarians do and what education they need. In fact it's troubling that after decades of trying to understand stereotypes and trying to defeat them, the public still has no idea what librarians do and what education they need.

In 2002, Fagan conducted a study of 48 undergraduates and discovered that, even when students considered librarians to be faculty, students still didn't know the amount of education required to be a librarian. They also thought librarian expertise was limited to the library's physical collection, and they included many clerical tasks in their descriptions of what librarians do. Overall, "students have a generally positive impression of librarians' attitudes toward them but aren't sure librarians are as willing to change services or to help during 'crunch time'" (p. 140). Kneale's (2009) survey from 2003 that was referenced earlier, which had 782 responses, also asked respondents if they think librarians need a degree to perform their job. 439 of the 782 respondents said "yes" while only 222 respondents said "no." She also asked patrons if they thought anyone who worked in a library was a librarian and only 69 respondents said "yes" while 593 respondents said "no." Kneale says this shows promise that patrons are finally understanding and appreciating our work. However in Majid and Haider's article from 2008, the survey respondents did not show the same level of understanding. Of the 214 respondents, "only 20 respondents believed that the nature of work done by librarians was professional. Instead the majority of them viewed the nature of librarians' work as administrative and clerical…This finding was in line with many previous studies where librarians' work was found to be not properly understood" (p. 234). The authors also said that only 6.5% of respondents thought a bachelor's degree was required for the job while only 1.9% of respondents thought a master's degree was required; however, as Majid and Haider point out, the level of perceived education is expected since most of the respondents didn't perceive librarianship as professional work (p. 235). Majid and Haider also asked about perceived level of computing knowledge and said, "It was somewhat surprising that accountants and teachers were perceived to possess better computing knowledge and skills than librarians. It was unexpected as Singapore libraries are well known for their prompt and innovative use of sophisticated technologies" (p. 236). Notice Majid and Haider said Singapore *libraries* are known for technology use, not Singapore *librarians*; patrons aren't making the connection between the technology offered by the library and the librarians' ability to use it. Majid and Haider go on to say, "It appeared that many respondents, as also revealed by many earlier studies, were unable to distinguish librarians from other library staff. This confusion is probably due to the apparent 'invisibility' of librarians to their users. In many libraries, users interact more frequently with para-professionals and counter clerks as these individuals…perform certain 'visible' tasks such as answering basic reference queries, performing circulation transactions, shelving library materials, maintaining equipment, and managing library security" (p. 239). Pagowsky and DeFrain's (2014) discussion of warmth versus competence and their citing articles that show even faculty members do not understand our abilities is further evidence to suggest that people don't know exactly what it is librarians do or what they are capable of doing; by extension, of course people will not truly understand the required level of education.

Despite the mixed reviews the literature gives us about public perceptions of librarians, the Pew Research Center's data shows stereotypes are not stopping people from utilizing and valuing library services, in this case public library services; however it does show that patrons don't fully understand public library services. According to the data from surveys of Americans ages 16 and older, 95% "agree that the materials and resources available at public libraries play an important role in giving everyone a chance to succeed; 95% say that public libraries are important because they promote literacy and a love of reading; 94% say that having a public library improves the quality of life in a community;"

and "81% say that public libraries provide many services people would have a hard time finding elsewhere" (Zickhur, Rainie, Purcell, & Duggan, 2013, "The Importance of Public Libraries to Their Communities," para. 2). The survey also shows that, among all Americans who have ever used a public library, "94% said that based on their own experiences, they would say that 'public libraries are welcoming, friendly places,'" and "91% said that they personally have never had a negative experience using a public library, either in person or online" (Zickhur et al., 2013, "Most Americans…Positive Experiences," para. 1). Finally, while the survey revealed libraries are easily accessible to most Americans and they know the location of their public libraries, "23% of those who have ever used a public library said they feel like they know all or most of the services and programs their library offers, while a plurality (47%) said that they know some of what it offers. About one in five (20%) say they don't know very much about what is offered, and 10% say they know 'nothing at all'" (Zickhur et al., 2013, "Most Americans Know Where their Local Library Is," para. 2). These statistics about knowing what services a library offers are troubling — the majority of library users do not have a clear idea of the services the library offers, and they are already using the library. Although they have everyone who used a public library lumped together as opposed to breaking it down to heavy users versus occasional users, it's certainly not difficult to understand why people who don't use libraries fail to see their value.

    While the research does show promising data, it is discouraging to see that after decades of examining library stereotypes and trying to change them, we are still falling short. It seems like our efforts thus far to combat stereotypes and to help people understand what we do is not actually producing the results we would like it to.

CHAPTER 7

Librarians and Stereotypes Survey

The research thus far has examined librarian representations and public perceptions of librarians, but what's lacking is a look at what we as librarians think about patron perceptions of us and the profession. What do we think are the stereotypes people have? Are we seeing new stereotypes evolving? Do these stereotypes impact us professionally and personally? And, if we think it's up to librarians to change stereotypes, do we think we actually are changing the stereotypes? With this survey the author hopes to gain some insight into the aforementioned questions in order to determine whether or not our efforts to improve stereotypes have been, or can ever truly be, effective.

Background

In summer 2014, the author of this book, who is also the researcher for this study, created a survey/questionnaire that contained 25 questions; two questions related to reading disclosure statements, and 23 questions related to the content of the study. The survey contained a mix of multiple choice, short answer, and multiple select questions; it can be found in Appendix A. The survey, which was completed anonymously, was administered online via Google forms, and no computer I.P. addresses were saved by the author or used to trace responses back to anyone. A disclosure statement told participants they were not encouraged or required to share any information that could personally identify them in any of the responses. Participants were able to opt out of the survey by clicking off of the form without submitting any information, and participants could also skip questions. This project did not require Institutional Review Board (IRB) approval because it was done independently of any institution and federal funding; however, in the interest of research ethics, the researcher still looked into obtaining IRB approval. Because the researcher's institution did not have an IRB and because it was cost prohibitive to obtain outside IRB approval, the researcher did not obtain IRB approval. The author did, however, informally speak with people who sit on IRB boards and thoroughly reviewed the Office for Human Research and Protection's (2004) decision trees to be absolutely certain this study did not require IRB approval. Also, in the interest of research ethics, the researcher did not conduct research in any manner that would fall under IRB approval requirements if the project was receiving funding. Finally, the researcher made sure the study adhered to the Belmont Report's ethical principles for research involving human subjects: "respect for persons" (participants had the right to decline participation or to drop out later), "beneficence" ("do no harm"), and "justice" (participants were treated fairly) (Burns and Grove, 2009, p. 188).

Researcher Interests

The researcher of this study is a librarian at a small nursing school in northeastern Pennsylvania. The researcher has a background in public relations and communication studies with an interest in gender studies. She has dealt with librarian stereotypes both inside and outside of work since deciding to become a librarian, and this led to an interest in librarian representations and how they impact perceptions of the profession. Particularly, coming from a public relations background, she was concerned with how we choose to represent ourselves and how that impacts the profession, whether that impact is positive or negative.

Methodology

This study is qualitative in nature. According to Leedy and Ormrod (2005), "some qualitative researchers believe that there isn't necessarily a single, ultimate Truth to be discovered. Instead, there may be multiple perspectives held by different individuals;" thus "as a general rule, qualitative studies do not allow the researcher to identify cause-effect relationships" (p. 133, 135). The researcher agrees with this — there is no single, correct answer to many issues, particularly when it comes to stereotypes. Because it's not possible to determine one specific factor that caused the stereotypes we have now, it's impossible to determine a cause-effect relationship. The researcher made observations about possible causes and effects through the frameworks of critical social theory, symbolic interaction theory, and phenomenology.

Critical Social Theory

"Critical social theorists are critical of what they see as pervasive inequalities and injustices in everyday relationships and arrangements. They view society as a human construction in need of reconstruction." Critical social theory "brings together multiple beliefs about human understanding and misunderstanding, the nature of change, and the role of critique and education in society" (Freeman & Vasconcelos, 2010, p. 7). Freeman and Vasconcelos add that "central to a critical theory argument is that systems…produce knowledge in such a way as to obscure their oppressive consequences. Unjust practices and arrangements, therefore, do not manifest themselves in straightforward ways but become distorted and hidden over time within contextually and culturally embedded practices (Dant, 2003)" (p. 8). Because the stereotypes related to librarians are rooted in our cultural ideals of gender, in our psychology, and in our communication, critical social theory is a natural theoretical framework to use. Finally, Freeman and Vasconcelos (2010) tell us, "embedded in all critical social theories are four interrelated theories (Fay, 1987, pp. 31-32), which we paraphrase in our own words: (a) a theory of false consciousness, which explains the nature and process through which social members' values and beliefs become obscured and distorted by dominant ideologies, (b) a theory of crisis, which locates and describes the source and nature of oppression in question, (c) a theory of education, which accounts for the conditions and processes necessary for enlightenment or alternate visions to surface, and (d) a theory of transformative action, which details the kinds of actions and alterations needed to resolve the identified crisis" (pp. 11-12). In fact this false consciousness can account for self-objectification; in self-objectification, women internalize their oppression and perpetuate it by objectifying themselves and other women.

Symbolic Interaction Theory (Symbolic Interactionism)

The concept of symbolic interaction spans many social science disciplines. Critical social theory examines the inequalities in life and how the system maintains these inequalities, and symbolic interaction offers insight into how these inequalities are created and maintained. Symbolic interactionists believe we create our identities socially — we need other people to determine who we are and who we should be.

According to Brinkerhoff et al. (2005), symbolic interaction theory begins with four premises: "To understand human behaviors, we must first understand what those behaviors mean to the individual actors. Those meanings develop within social relationships and roles. Individuals actively construct their self-concepts. However, social structure and social roles limit our options for constructing our self-concepts." Individuals construct their identities via a process of three concepts — the looking-glass self in which we imagine what others think about us, role taking in which we put ourselves in the roles of the others to determine the criteria used to judge ourselves, and role identity which is "the image we have of ourselves in a specific social role" (p. 60-61).

The researcher wanted to determine what librarians think are the stereotypes and how librarians are working to change them; thus the context of this survey is librarians socially constructing their identities, and symbolic interaction is appropriate.

Phenomenology

In addition to using critical social theory and symbolic interaction, the researcher used a phenomenological study to gather data. Leedy and Ormrod (2005) explain phenomenology: "In its broadest sense, the term *phenomenology* refers to a person's perception of the meaning of an event, as opposed to the event as it exists external to the person. A phenomenological study is a study that attempts to understand people's perceptions, perspectives, and understandings of a particular situation" (p. 139). Because the purpose of this study was to determine what librarians thought about stereotypes and their self-representations, a phenomenological study was appropriate.

Method of Administration

The researcher used Google forms to create a 25 question anonymous survey; this survey was actually more of a questionnaire because it solicited so many short answer responses that were similar to interview questions in addition to multiple choice and multiple select questions. According to Burns and Grove (2009), "a questionnaire is a printed self-report form designed to illicit information that can be obtained from a subject's written responses. The information derived through a questionnaire is similar to that obtained by interview" (p. 406).

The researcher utilized a convenience sample for this project, and she chose her participants via purposive sampling and snowballing in order to ensure librarians at a variety of stages in their careers from a variety of libraries across the United States received the survey; the researcher sent the survey to 97 librarian colleagues and asked them to forward the information if they wanted to do so. One colleague responded that he forwarded the survey to 11 of his colleagues. Because it was not required for the researcher's colleagues to tell her if they sent the survey and to how many people, it is impossible to determine the number of people who actually received the survey; however, it is certain that at least 108 librarians received the survey.

The researcher developed her own survey but did not do pilot testing. Despite the lack of pilot testing, the researcher believes her survey provided an accurate picture of librarians' views of stereotypes because all but the demographic questions specifically focused on the presentation of self in relation to stereotypes. The survey was also the same for everyone and was administered the same way — regardless of whether or not the participant received the survey directly from the researcher or from a colleague, the Google form link included in the email linked everyone to the same survey that contained the same instructions and information for everyone. Those who chose to complete the survey did so anonymously online, and responses could not be altered once they were submitted. Clearly there was little if any chance of bias, and anonymity gave participants the ability to answer questions freely and honestly.

Because the author was staying within the guidelines of research that did not require IRB approval, she did not ask respondents to participate in any personal interviews about their experiences.

A letter inviting librarians to participate in the research was emailed on August 17, 2014. At that time, anyone who declined to participate was removed from the survey email list. The survey was emailed on August 19, 2014, and participants had one month to complete it. Two weeks after the initial email was sent, a reminder email containing the same information as the initial email was sent to participants. The survey closed on September 19, 2014.

This survey was sent to colleagues in the library and information science profession; their job title did not need to be "librarian" in order to complete the survey, but their work had to be librarian work according to the U.S. Bureau of Labor Statistics' Occupational Handbook (2014): a librarian is someone who helps "people find information and conduct research for personal and professional use. Their job duties may be based on the type of library they work in" but include helping library patrons find resources and conduct searches, teaching information literacy classes, organizing collections, planning programs, indexing materials, collection development, preparing library budgets, training library employees, and providing reference services" (para. 1–2). This definition was included in the survey's introduction.

The survey was completed via Google Forms which allowed all responses to be exported to an Excel spreadsheet. The author was then able to analyze the responses and create visual depictions of them. For the short answer questions, the author reviewed the comments and assigned codes in order to categorize them. Each short answer question could contain multiple comments, so the comments were coded into comprehensive categories and the code categories were tallied based on the number of times they appeared in the responses.

Quality of the Study

The method fits the parameters of a phenomenological study according to Leedy and Ormrod (2005): In phenomenology, "the central task during data analysis is to identify common themes in people's descriptions of their experiences (Barritt, 1986)…The researcher typically takes the following steps (Cresswell, 1998): (1) Identify statements that relate to the topic… (2) Group statements into 'meaning units'… (3) Seek divergent perspectives… (4) Construct a composite. The researcher uses the various meanings identified to develop an overall description of the phenomenon as people typically experience it" (as cited in Leedy and Ormrod, 2005, p. 140).

The researcher believes this study also met the standards of a good qualitative study. While quantitative studies are based on reliability and validity, a number of other factors have been proposed to judge the quality of qualitative studies. Leedy and Ormrod (2005) looked at the various criteria and

> "boiled the suggestions down to nine general criteria: (1) Purposefulness. The research question drives the methods used… (2) Explicitness of assumptions and biases. The researcher identifies and communicates any assumptions, beliefs, values, and biases that may influence data collection and interpretation. (3) Rigor. The researcher used rigorous, precise, and thorough methods to collect, record, and analyze data…(4) Open-mindedness. The researcher shows willingness to modify hypotheses and interpretations when newly acquired data conflicts with previously collected data. (5) Completeness. The researcher depicts the object of study in all its complexity… (6) Coherence. The data yield consistent findings, such that the researcher can

present a portrait that 'hangs together.' Multiple data sources converge onto consistent conclusions (triangulation), and any contradictions within the data are reconciled. (7) Persuasiveness. The researcher presents logical arguments... (8) Consensus. Other individuals, including the participants in the study and other scholars in the discipline, agree with the researcher's interpretations and examinations. (9) Usefulness. The project yields conclusions that promote better understanding of the phenomenon, enable more accurate predictions about future events, or lead to interventions that enhance the quality of life" (pp. 154-155).

The researcher believes the study meets these standards in the following ways because the research question informed the framework and the methods; the researcher was cognizant of her assumptions and biases and has revealed these in the "researcher interests" section; the survey contains a variety of question types, its sample was purposeful, and it was anonymous; the researcher did not come into the study with a hypothesis in mind but instead was open-minded; and the survey examines multiple aspects of the topic.

Results

Of the 108 surveys that were sent out, only 32 respondents completed and submitted their surveys. Survey respondents were primarily older in age — 75% were 36 years old and older (see Figure 1) — and were overwhelmingly female (female = 71.88%, male = 28.12%). Despite 75% of the respondents being older, only 34.39% of the respondents had 11 or more years in the profession; thus it is likely librarianship was not the first career for many respondents. Figure 2 shows a comparison of librarian age and time in the profession.

Figure 1: Ages of Librarians

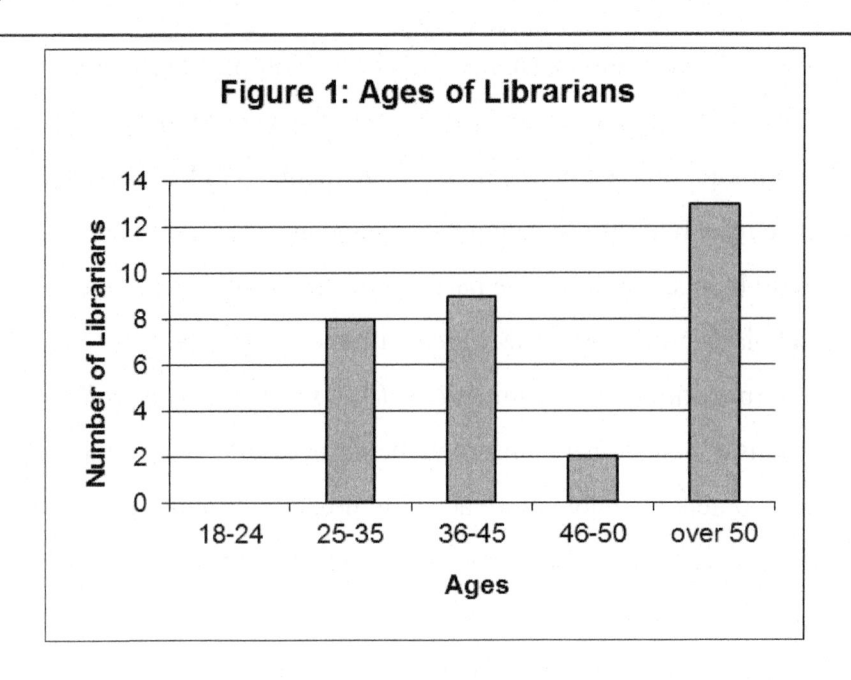

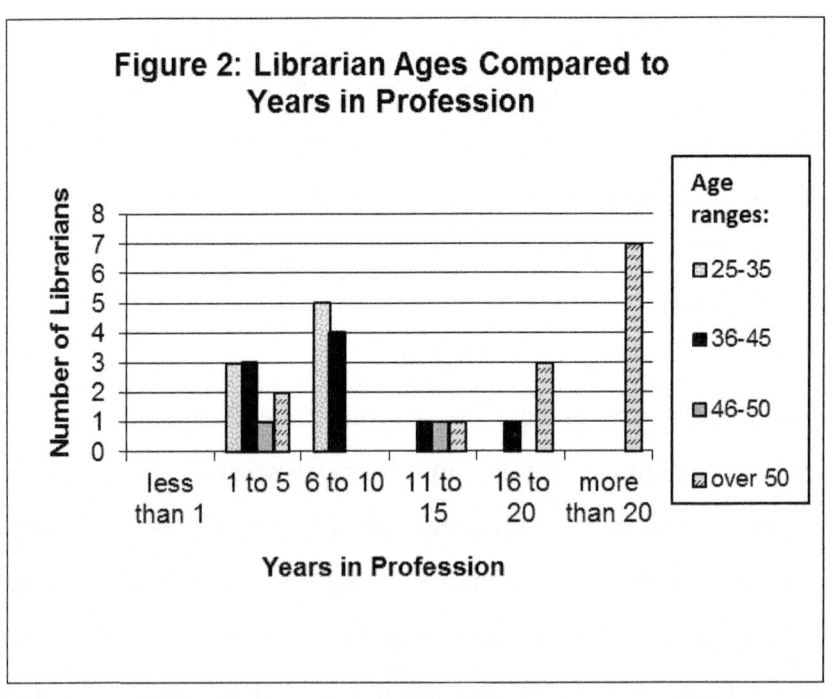

Figure 2: Librarian Ages Compared to Years in Profession

Note that the 18-24 year old age range is omitted because there were no 18-24 year old respondents.

Different types of librarians were represented, but they were not represented equally: 62.5% were academic librarians, 25% were public librarians, 9.38% were special librarians, and one respondent classified him/herself as working in an "other" type of library; no school librarians were represented.

When asked about their public (openly accessible to anyone; without privacy restrictions), online presence, 84.37% of respondents said they have some kind of public, online presence. Of those respondents, 92.6% said this presence identifies them as a librarian or their appropriate job title. Also, of the respondents with a public online presence, 66.67% share both personal and professional information while 33.33% share just professional information. Figure 3 shows a detailed breakdown of where the respondents have their public, online presences.

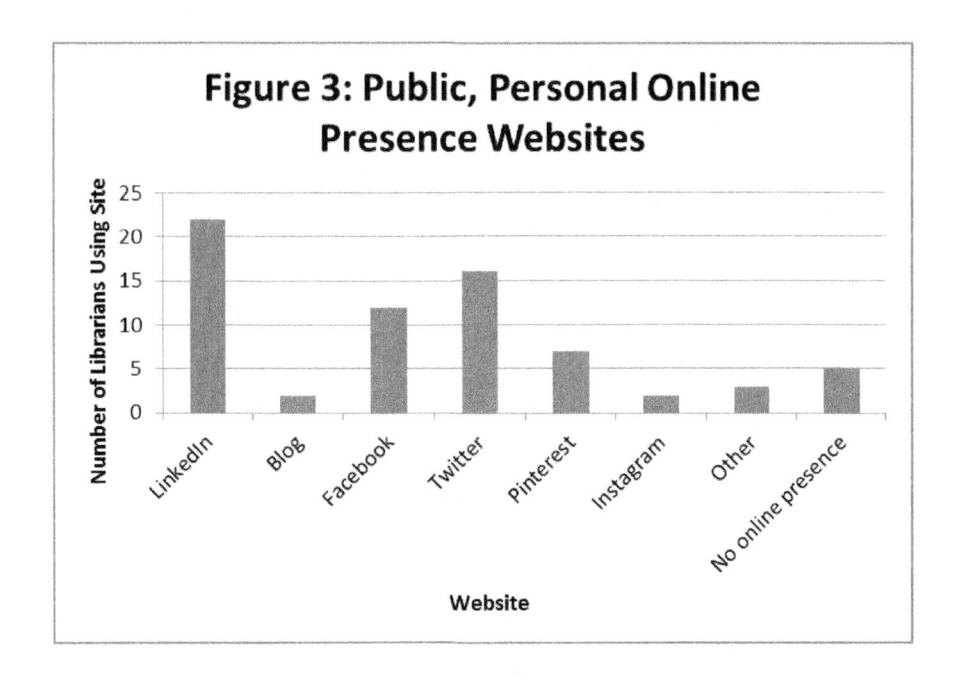

Figure 3: Public, Personal Online Presence Websites

Respondents were also asked to reflect on whether or not they consciously consider librarian stereotypes when choosing their wardrobe and accessories for work (yes = 43.75%; no = 56.25%) and for outside of work (yes = 18.75%; no = 81.25%). They were also asked to consider whether or not they consciously considered librarian stereotypes when interacting with people online and face to face at work (yes = 37.5%; no = 62.5%) and outside of work (yes = 31.25%; no = 68.75%). The results of these questions are depicted in Figure 4. It's interesting to see that more respondents thought about stereotypes when choosing their wardrobe and accessories for work than when interacting with people at work. It is also interesting to see how the results are nearly the same for both questions. These responses to the multiple choice matrix appear to indicate that respondents do not overwhelmingly consider librarian stereotypes when making decisions about how to present themselves; however, the short answer responses, which were worded in more specific ways, contradict this assumption.

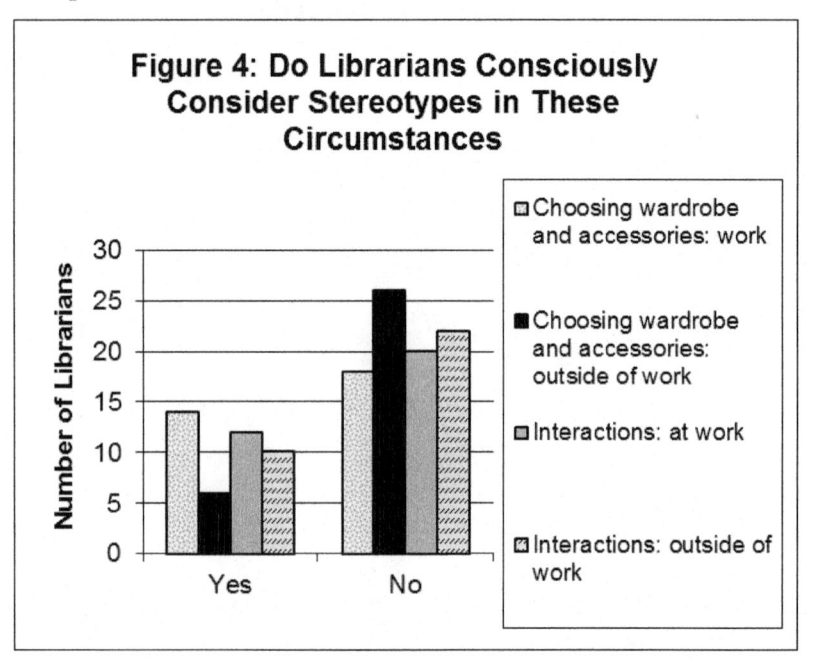

Figure 4: Do Librarians Consciously Consider Stereotypes in These Circumstances

Participants were asked, "Do you intentionally, in person and/or online, try to present yourself in a way that disproves any librarian stereotypes?," and were asked to use the space to respond "Yes" or "No" and to explain their answer. Only 20 respondents answered this question and, of those 20 respondents, 75% said yes, they do intentionally try to present themselves in a way that disproves librarian stereotypes. Comments include:

- "I have pretty much always tried to de-bunk the old lady librarian-shush idea."
- "I am anti-frump."
- "I try to present myself as very approachable, laid back, fun, and up to date with popular culture, and definitely not concerned about noise in the library! I also am careful about not wearing my hear in a bun, wearing heavy glasses, or cardigans, or dressing in a way that might suggest the 'sexy librarian' look."

Comments for those who responded "No" to this question include:

- "Librarian stereotypes do not guide my behavior. Professionalism guides my behavior at work."
- "I am a dynamic individual. I present me for me, not in response to any perceived or real stereotypes about my career."
- "I don't (consciously) try to portray myself with respect to traditional librarian stereotypes. I do try to convey an attitude of 'approachable professionalism.'"

Participants were also asked if they consciously tried to present themselves — either in person or online — in ways that invoke any librarian stereotype, and they were again asked to explain their answers.

Again, 20 respondents answered this question; 20% said yes, they do try to invoke stereotypes, while 70% said no, they do not; 10% gave answers that did not address the question. Comments for those who responded "Yes" include:

- "I frequently invoke the stereotype of the librarian as a person who knows how to find answers to any and all questions. In response to someone who says, 'Wow, how do you know that?,' I proudly respond, 'I'm a librarian.'"
- "Only that I love books."

Comments for those who responded "No" include:

- "I do not intentionally present myself as a librarian stereotype because that has negative connotations, especially if it makes the patron feel inferior. I portray someone who is happy to assist patrons in any way."
- "I don't have any interest in invoking stereotypes. I do strive to present myself as professional, knowledgeable, and intelligent."
- "I want people to see me, not my job."

Following the questions about consciously defying or invoking stereotypes, participants were asked why they represent themselves the way they do in public, both in person and online. Twenty four people responded to this question. The majority of the comments — their tallied numbers are presented in parentheses — focused on being seen as a competent professional (8), being approachable (6), and disrupting expectations/dispelling stereotypes (6). See Table 1 for more information.

Participants were then asked how they think stereotypes impact a librarian's ability to do his or her job. Coded responses are summarized in

Table 2, but the majority of comments focused on how negative stereotypes impact the ability to do the job. For example, stereotypes lead to barriers to librarian effectiveness, reduced approachability, and an internal struggle for librarians; they struggle between being themselves and conforming to stereotypes. Comments also touched on reduced funding and staffing and a negative impact on salaries. Some comments did mention stereotypes not having an impact, and some mentioned more positive impacts such as being seen as knowledgeable and being approachable.

Table 1: Why do you represent yourself this way?

Show librarians as competent professionals	8
Be approachable	6
Disrupt expectations/dispel stereotypes	6
Be myself	4
Show profession in a positive light/improve image	2
Mock stereotype	2
Don't want to share too much/want to stay moderate	2

Table 2: How do you think stereotypes impact a librarian's ability to do the job?

Present barriers to effectiveness (i.e. community attitudes)	7
Negative impact on salaries/resources/funding/advancement	5
No impact	4
Difficult to prove our value	3
Reduce our approachability	2
We see ourselves as passive/reactive	1
Gender bias leads to stereotypes of our knowledge	1
They prove we are knowledgeable	1
Increase our approachability	1
Show our value	1
Struggle to be ourselves vs. to conform	1

In addition to these questions, participants were asked how they think stereotypes influence our personalities once we become librarians. Twenty one people responded to this question, and 47.62% of respondents' comments said there was either no influence or very little influence. Comments from the rest of the respondents mentioned a variety of positive and negative influences such as making librarians more outgoing and making us defensive. All of the comments were coded and are represented in Table 3.

Table 3: How do you think stereotypes impact our personalities once we become librarians?

No impact/minimal impact	10
We become defensive/ ready to defy stereotypes	5
They make us be more helpful to patrons.	3
We use them as icebreakers with patrons.	1
They make us aggressive leaders.	1
It depends on whether the stereotypes are positive or negative.	1
We imitate those in our profession – we have internal stereotypes to conform to.	1
We become frustrated with them.	1
We try too hard to be funny.	1
We feel pressure to conform to some of them.	1

When asked whether they think the patrons they serve have a generally positive, generally negative, or generally neutral view of the library/librarians, 31 people responded: 68.75% said they thought their patrons had a generally positive view of the profession while 25% thought the view was generally neutral. No one thought their patrons had a generally negative view, but one person was unsure of patron views. Thirty-one people responded to the question that asked what they think the views of the overall public are: 56.25% thought the views of the public were generally positive and 25% thought they were generally neutral. In this case, 2 respondents thought the public's views were generally negative while 3 respondents were unsure. The short answer section, however, showed librarians believe the public has more negative views.

When asked, "How do you think stereotypes impact public perceptions of librarians/librarianship?" (a question which 23 respondents answered), 5 comments contained views that were not positive, even if they were not exactly negative. These comments mentioned library anxiety, perceptions generally tending to be negative, and the "weak, passive librarian" stereotype. Three comments showed opinions that the public thinks librarians and librarianship are replaceable by the Internet, and another 3 comments referred to librarians being seen as primarily working with books and being "bookworms" who are "not to be modern." Only 5 comments included definitively positive thoughts about how stereotypes have impacted public perceptions. These comments dealt with librarians being knowledgeable and being public servants. Seven comments revealed that respondents think the public does not have a clear idea of what librarians do. Results are summarized in Table 4.

Table 4: How do you think stereotypes impact public perceptions?

Make the public unsure of what we do and know	7
They do not lead to positive views.	5
Show we are replaceable by Internet	3
Portray us as working with and/or loving books	3
They define the public's expectations of us.	3
Not much impact/no impact	2
Depends on the stereotype	2
Public sees us as knowledgeable	2
Librarians seen as public servants	1
Unsure	1
Public perceptions from stereotypes can be changed with librarian interaction.	1

When asked what types of stereotypes they think people currently associate with librarians, participants gave a variety of responses. Most of the 28 people who responded to this question listed characteristics as opposed to citing stereotype categories mentioned in the literature; however three categories from the literature were cited in comments — the old maid (2 comments), the sexy librarian (2 comments), and the hero (1 comment). Characteristics that fit with the old maid stereotype were also mentioned: glasses (3), stickler for the rules/shushing (2), mean (2), middle age or older woman (2), cling to or at least prefer print (2), and buns (1). One comment mentioned sexually repressed, which would fit both the old maid and the sexy librarian stereotype. Other characteristics mentioned were: "bookish" — like to read and work with books (10), conservative/boring (9), quiet and reserved (8), female (6), poorly dressed — includes wearing sensible shoes (2), and white (1). Respondents also pointed out the fact that librarian work and education is often misunderstood (4) as well as the fact that patrons think everyone who works in a library is a librarian (2). Positive stereotypes were mentioned as well. In fact the comment that mentioned "heroic" also said, "Now librarians are seen as kind of heroic and as standards bearers for accuracy, rationality, balance, determination, equality, and technological expertise, keepers of our collective past but explorers of the emerging future."

In addition to positive and negative stereotypes, respondents mentioned two other emerging stereotypes — nerdy (5) and cat lovers (4). At this time, both of these stereotypes appear to be neutral. The nerdy stereotype invokes intelligence but could end up negative because traditionally being called a nerd or nerdy was meant as an insult. However, at this time, society has an affinity for shows featuring smart or nerdy characters and for the "geek chic" clothing trend, so this could be a positive librarian stereotype for the time being. The cat lover stereotype has been associated with cute depictions of library cats and librarians with cats, so it has not yet crossed into negative territory and become a "crazy cat lady" association.

Despite the fact that there were a variety of positive, negative, and neutral responses, the majority of responses were either neutral or negative; there were too many responses to list here, but the top 10 responses are summarized in Table 5. This seems to conflict with the earlier multiple choice question about whether the respondents think the public overall has generally positive, negative, or neutral views on libraries and librarianship; in that question, respondents thought the views of the public were generally positive or neutral.

Table 5: Top 10 Responses to What Stereotypes Librarians Think Exist About Profession

"Bookish"- likes to read/ work with books	10
Conservative/boring	9
Quiet/reserved	8
Smart/knowledgeable	6
Female	6
Helpful	5
Nerdy	5
Love cats	4
Wear glasses	3
Orderly/organized	3

Negative stereotypes impact the profession, however positive and neutral stereotypes may impact the profession as well; thus the participants were asked what impact they think positive and neutral stereotypes have on the profession. Twenty five respondents answered this question. While many of the comments focused on positive impacts such as increased utilization of the library (4) and demonstrating our skills and abilities (2),

2 comments stated the respondents were unsure, 1 comment noted neutral stereotypes can become negative, and 1 comment noted that positive and/or neutral stereotypes can lead to internal divisions among those in the library who do and don't fit those stereotypes. Overall, though, most comments mentioned positive impacts. See Table 6 for a summary of the coded responses.

Table 6: How do you think positive/neutral stereotypes impact the profession?

Improved funding/perceptions/public support	4
People will utilize library	4
Empower us and encourage professional growth	3
Improves recruitment/LIS program enrollment	3
Impacts respect/salaries	2
Demonstrate our skills/abilities	2
Unsure	2
Profession survives	2
Non-response/unable to code	2
Neutral could end up negative	1
Help us maintain the public's trust	1
No impact	1
Lead to internal divisions	1

Participants were also asked how they think stereotypes impact people's desire to become librarians; 22 people responded to this question. As you can see from Table 7, the majority of comments mention a negative impact on recruitment. Only 2 comments relate to stereotypes encouraging people to enter the profession while 2 comments showed respondents' beliefs that the impact depends on the stereotype. One comment mentioned librarian influence also impacts this decision. Librarian influence is an important point that should not be overlooked. Ultimately the decision to become a librarian, and any decisions related to library use, depends on a combination of stereotypes and librarian influence; this is why librarians worry so much about stereotypes and their resultant perceptions — negative stereotypes often lead people to avoid the library, and this avoidance means they will never get the chance to have that librarian influence which could offset negative stereotypes.

Table 7: How do you think stereotypes impact people's desire to become librarians?

Drives people away/people think it's outdated	9
People attracted to profession for wrong reasons/profession doesn't attract qualified candidates	5
No impact/minimal impact	3
Librarian influence matters	2
Depends on the stereotype	2
Positive stereotypes encourage people to join profession for right reasons	2
Unsure	1

When asked how librarians can combat negative stereotypes, comments from the 23 people who responded to this question primarily focused on demonstrating skills and abilities (9) and being proactive with outreach (6). Comments also related to librarians challenging and/or confronting stereotypes when they are presented with them during interactions (5), but no one proposed challenging the stereotypes without the patron first presenting them. In fact 1 comment suggested ignoring stereotypes while 2 comments said librarians shouldn't combat negative stereotypes. The responses are summarized in Table 8.

Finally, participants were asked what they hoped their representations of themselves, either online or in person, do for the image of librarianship. While 2 respondents said they hadn't given this any thought, the majority of comments showed respondents hope their self-representations show librarians are competent professionals (7), helpful and knowledgeable (7), and valuable (6), and they hope their self-representations help people see the profession in a positive light (4). See Table 9 for more information.

Table 8: How can librarians combat negative stereotypes?

Demonstrate your skills/abilities	9
Be proactive with outreach	6
Challenge/correct stereotypes when they are presented	5
Do your job well	3
Be yourself	3
Not responsible for this/no need to do this	2
Believe in your skills/abilities	2
Take profession seriously/Don't "talk down" about it.	2
Acquire necessary skills	2
Ignore stereotypes	1
Use facts to back up why your services are important	1
Dress well	1

Table 9: What do you hope your representations of yourself do for the profession?

Show librarians are competent professionals	7
Show we are helpful/ knowledgeable	7
Haven't thought about it/ Unsure	3
Show we are valuable	6
Show the profession in a positive light	4
Show us as educators	2
No impact	2
Discourage stereotypes	2
Show we are adaptable	1
I don't try to do anything for the profession's image.	1
Show me as an individual.	1

Limitations

The study provides insight into librarians' thoughts on public perceptions and stereotypes, but it has limitations. The most limiting obstacle was the researcher's desire to work within the restrictions on human subject research that does not require IRB approval. Follow up research should obtain IRB approval, or at the very least informed consent if the researcher is still working completely independently, in order to have in-depth follow up interviews with respondents. Another limitation is using a convenience sample as opposed to a larger, more generalizable sample. A true random sampling would have been difficult to obtain and would have required access to multiple library listservs across the United States; the researcher did not have this access. Although a convenience sample is a limitation, the author engaged in purposive sampling to make sure librarians from all types of libraries across the country who varied in age, were at various stages in their careers, and worked in a variety of libraries were represented. The low response rate — approximately 29.63% — is another limitation, especially since the small response rate did not include an equal amount of respondents from different types of libraries. However Burns and Grove (2009) explain, "the response rate for questionnaires is usually small (25% to 30%)" (p. 409). Although this limits the ability to generalize the results, the ultimate aim of qualitative research is not generalize results but to describe the phenomenon at hand. Still, a higher response rate would've led to greater accuracy when describing the phenomenon. The low response rate could be attributed to topic fatigue — librarian stereotypes are frequently studied and, despite the fact that this is a new angle on the topic, librarians may not have wanted to participate in more research regarding stereotypes. Also, the length of the survey may have been a factor in the low response rate; half of the questions on the survey were short answer questions that required reflection. Finally, the time of year the survey was administered may have been an issue. The survey was administered mid-August through mid-September because this time frame seemed to conflict the least with conferences, vacations and holidays, and workloads across the different areas of librarianship. Perhaps sending the survey to librarians in specific fields at different times of the year, times that were better for that specific field, would have returned better results.

Discussion and Future Research

The research in this study had its limitations, but it provided valid points for discussion and for future research. The first noticeable point is that there was a discrepancy between what respondents chose in the multiple select matrix and what they wrote in the short answer questions. While it's not possible to do a true one-to-one comparison between them because every respondent did not answer the short answer questions, it is clear that stereotypes are there, at least subconsciously, even if we don't care about them. A survey that is not anonymous and would allow for follow up questions to clarify these discrepancies is warranted.

The current survey looked at librarianship as a whole and it showed that, across the three major areas of librarianship represented by the respondents, the stereotypes seem to be present and consistent. However, surveys that look at stereotypes as applied to each field of librarianship separately would give a more accurate picture of stereotypes and the profession because different areas of librarianship may differ substantially. For example, public libraries serve the general public and their services may or may not be viewed as necessary to the patrons they serve; on the other hand, medical libraries primarily serve physicians, nurses, and other clinical care specialists and the services offered by these librarians may be seen as essential for evidence-based healthcare. Thus the public served by public libraries and the public served by medical libraries may differ substantially on how they view librarians as well as the libraries and the necessity of their services.

The current research also revealed the need for librarianship to examine stereotypes through the lenses of other fields. The research shows this because short answer responses revealed that librarians still think the public sees us as old maids who can't do much to help it. This is cause for concern because it means that despite our best efforts at rebranding ourselves and our services after all of these decades of "navel gazing," we are still failing to portray ourselves in a different light. Why is that? Also, it must be made clear that despite the abundance of literature surrounding stereotypes over the past number of decades, and despite some of the survey respondents' thoughts to the contrary, it is still important to examine stereotypes so we can better combat them. Whether we like it or not, stereotypes impact our funding, staffing, utilization of services, and our future. As one survey respondent mentioned, "Each librarian has the ability to help all other librarians overcome stereotypes. Even though some think our dress or behavior should not matter, even if it should not, it does; and therefore, I believe, all librarians should be cognizant of helping the profession."

In response to the aforementioned question about stereotypes impacting a person's desire to become a librarian, one of the respondents suggested, "Perhaps we should ask college students this question." Posing this question to college students is something that should be done in the future, but posing this question to high school students who are beginning career exploration in preparation for college would also be beneficial. As far as posing the question to college students, asking students at a variety of stages in their decision making process for their major would be beneficial. It would also be beneficial to ask library science students who are beginning their program of study why they chose this field, asking those who do not complete the program why they did not complete it, and asking those who graduate if their views about the profession changed throughout their program.

Library science degrees are versatile, and changes in the economy have forced some people with library science degrees to find employment outside of traditional library fields. An interesting study would be to ask those who work outside of traditional library fields why they chose this field (not all of them were forced into non-traditional fields because of the economy), how their degree is applicable, and reactions from colleagues when they learn these people went to school for library science.

If we fail to realize the importance of stereotypes and their impact on the profession and we fail to figure out why our efforts are failing, or if we at least fail to figure out what stereotypes are realistic to change, we will find the profession in an even more grim state.

CHAPTER 8

So, Now What?

The book has presented an overview of the popular librarian stereotypes that have been described in literature, and the survey has provided insight into what stereotypes librarians think still exist. It seems the most prevalent are the old maid and the sexy librarian, and we see cat loving librarians and nerdy librarians emerging as new stereotypes. The news media also like to portray hipster librarians. Thus it seems not much is changing — the old maid is still there, the sexy librarian is still there and is becoming more present, and we are simply adding more stereotypes rather than shedding them. Our efforts haven't done much to improve the image of librarians, and the path we are currently on could be detrimental to the profession. In fact Roberto (2014) points out troubling emerging trends: "These days, it appears that the most prevalent librarian archetypes embrace fandoms and a certain type of detail-oriented geekiness, the latter being a favorite in library land" ("I Was a Hipster," para. 1). Roberto adds, "The images that we currently prize are those that celebrate our arcane knowledge as opposed to our useful skills, ultimately arguing for an expert-based model instead of a service-based one" ("I Was a Hipster," para. 1). This image borders on becoming a know it all librarian who still isn't any more necessary than Google. If all a librarian can do is spout arcane knowledge, what good is he or she? Google can, theoretically, do the same thing without making the patron feel inferior. While it's nice to know we are seen as knowledgeable, we must also be seen as useful and necessary.

Roberto (2014) also points out, "Another eternally popular trend in library work is rampant technophilia…our digital love affair manages to accommodate self-conscious irony, and possibly outright nostalgia, for all things non-digital…It sometimes appears that the future librarian stereotype will be to venerate the past as a dead artifact, disparage all current technology, and yearn for a new future where all librarians are either CIOs or programmers or work in special collections" ("I Can't Tell if I'm Being," paras. 1-2). It is interesting to see the dichotomy Roberto discusses. On one hand, librarians have a digital love affair and want to have as much technology as possible while on the other hand they are nostalgic for the past and, by extension, print. This nostalgia for the past is also a nostalgia for the "simpler times," before technology supposedly made things more difficult. Yet these "simpler times" are romanticized in the minds of many new librarians because they never experienced these times to understand they were not, in fact, simpler. A card catalog may look nice and be remnant of our library's history, but it's hard to argue that it was easier or even better to use than an electronic catalog. It seems we are on a path to either be IT people or archivists, neither of which exemplifies the entire spectrum of library work.

While Roberto's thoughts have merit — there are librarians who are in love with digital and shun all other things while there are librarians who yearn for that simpler, non-digital time (we do know that technology hasn't made everything easier) and are passionate about protecting print collections because they know what they can offer — he ignores the reasons behind technophilia and nostalgia. Libraries must adopt the technology our patrons expect us to have and want to use, and, yes, this does make it seem like we are very technophilic. Our culture is technophilic now, so what choice do libraries have? If we want to remain relevant, we have to provide the services and technologies our patrons want. But in addition to adopting technology to please our patrons, we must also adopt technology that improves our workflow. Again, we often don't have a choice in this matter because we are forced to do more with less and that often translates into doing more work with less staff. Technology is necessary so we can focus on the public as opposed to the back end of library functions. Unfortunately, once the technology ball starts rolling, we often have no choice but to roll with it. Updates and changes to programs mean we are all on a constant learning curve and we may be forced to work with software changes that do not make things easier. Those are the times we are rightfully nostalgic. The simpler times we yearn for are not exclusively pre-technology days, they may just be the days when technology wasn't constantly changing. Technology also creates new challenges that were not there with print; these challenges may make us rightfully nostalgic. To use Roberto's reference to special collections, there was a time when special collections librarians only had to worry about preserving print or tangible materials. These materials won't disappear because someone removes them from a server, and technology to access them won't become obsolete because you don't often need technology to access them. Digital collections present access and preservation issues that are difficult to deal with, much more difficult than print collections, and digital collections are also being ruled by outdated copyright laws. Thus some nostalgia for print is clearly understandable.

    Although Roberto's discussion overlooks the cultural forces driving these changes, it does point to the need for a balance in the profession. We are librarians, not just CIOs or people working in special collections. Librarianship mandates knowledge that spans two worlds that, contrary to naysayers, will always co-exist — digital and print. Choosing to be knowledgeable in one area while ignoring the other can be detrimental to the profession; thus stereotypes that embrace the technophile librarian or the nostalgic librarian are both dangerous and must be avoided.

Clearly cultural forces drive our decisions and play an important part in future stereotypes that libraries and librarians may or may not embrace. Cultural forces have shaped our current stereotypes, and they will either help or hinder our abilities to shed negative stereotypes. The following examples are two major cultural forces that will impact our abilities to shed stereotypes. Following these examples are recommendations as to what we can do to be realistic about stereotypes and to change what we can change while making the future more positive for the profession.

Millennials, Gen Z, and Cultural Changes

With how deeply rooted stereotypes are in our culture, especially since stereotypes often stem from more deeply rooted gender and communication ideas, this author believes a cultural shift is necessary to overcome some of the stereotypes. One such shift may be happening now to help change what's perhaps the most damaging stereotypes — technological ineptitude and our desire and ability to only work with print.

While libraries may always be the realm of the old maid, Millennials have grown up at a time that spans traditional print library work and resources and 21st century library work and resources. Generation Z, the post-Millennial generation, hasn't experienced a time before 21st century libraries and technology, and really only knows what librarians used to do because of what it sees in movies or hears from others. For the most part, younger Millennials and those in Generation Z do not personally know what it means to have a card catalog, to see a librarian stamping books, or even to have to sign a card in the back of the book to check the book out. They certainly haven't grown up in the era of quiet libraries. Thus younger generations are coming of age in the midst of a cultural shift, and they themselves could be the cultural shift we need to shed the idea of the technologically inept, print-loving librarian. In the eyes of the younger generations, everyone uses technology. This could remove the "technologically inept" frame of reference, and without a frame of reference there is no stereotype. Unfortunately there's no guarantee this shift will erase the stereotype. The image of the technologically inept librarian could still be prevalent and, if it is, this will surely kill the profession as we know it.

If Millennials and Gen Zers come to believe that, in this age of technology skills being essential, librarians lack those skills, then the profession will not reap any benefits of a cultural shift. Instead librarians will come to be associated with skills that are so archaic they didn't even exist in the lifetimes of Millennials and Gen Zers. If librarians are associated with such archaic skills, the current younger generations will see no value in them. However it isn't just the perceived lack of technology skills that could harm the profession. As Roberto (2014) noted, the trend of librarians embracing their factual knowledge as opposed to their service skills could also lead these younger generations to see librarians as non-essential. These are the generations of instant access to information. They can look up the answer to a ready reference question as soon as they think of the question. Why ask a librarian when you can just Google it? These trends are troubling not just because they don't show us as useful information — not information technology — professionals, but because we seem to be unaware of how harmful they can be. It seems as though librarians are willing to embrace any stereotype as long as it disproves the old maid stereotype. We are so desperate to separate ourselves from the old maid "other" that we are willing to embrace stereotypes that still show us as essentially useless. But these generations won't need librarians for their arcane knowledge that makes them great *Jeopardy!* contestants; they will need librarians for help navigating the information landscape, and they will only know they need us if they know we can help them.

The Female Gender and Its Consequences

Attitudes toward women and their work is a major cultural barrier to overcoming some of the stereotypical views of the profession. It will most certainly take a major cultural shift to overcome these attitudes and their consequences; younger generations are already creating this cultural shift because they lack a frame of reference for women not taking part in the workforce outside of home; they don't live in a time when women are expected — or many times even able — to quit work when they get married and have children. These younger generations are also coming of age in a time when men are sharing more of the domestic chores and this sharing is being represented in the media, and they are seeing more jobs becoming less gendered (i.e. teaching and nursing). In fact in medical fields, scrubs are gender neutral and we see women and men dressed the same way. Also, nursing — a traditionally female profession — while still statistically predominantly female is growing in scope and responsibility to become just as valued as the traditionally male-dominated health professions. While these younger generations may be changing the tide of women in the workforce, there is still a history of cultural barriers related to work and gender to overcome.

Gaines (2014) tells us in relation to library stereotypes, "The main problem is not that there are negative stereotypes of librarians, but rather that these negative stereotypes stem from hackneyed ideas of what women are and what women do. To confront these stereotypes and their implications, what may be needed is a radical change in the way that society views work" (para. 2). While Gaines is right — we must change the views we have of work — the roots of these views lie in our beliefs about gender. What is truly needed in society is a change in the way we view gender because our views about gender greatly impact our views about work. These intertwining views lead to stereotypes. For example, although women are gaining ground in the sciences, there is still some disbelief that they can be in engineering particularly if they meet society's standards of beauty. A recent event demonstrated this view that in the U.S., pretty women are not software engineers; instead the "tech and science industry" is "too often associated with the image of a white, geeky" male. Engineer Isis Wenger, who is a young woman that society considers beautiful, was featured on an advertisement for her company. The responses to the ad, rather than being happy that a woman was in software engineering, were sexist and wondered if people "buy into this image of what a female software engineer looks like." Wenger then took to Twitter posting pictures of herself and encouraging others to do the same with the hashtag #ILookLikeAnEngineer to help shed the stereotypical view of those working in science and technology (Tan, 2015). Science and technology is still a predominantly male field, but should women ever be equally represented in the field it will be interesting to see if the field follows the same path of devaluation as clerical work and librarianship followed. Clearly a change in the way we view gender would lead to a change in the way we view work because either 1) we won't feel the need to classify something as women's work or as men's work, or 2) work classified as women's work will no longer be devalued. Regardless of which change occurs, librarianship would garner more respect.

But is it truly possible to have a cultural shift in the way we view gender and its resultant gender norms? After all, it seems that throughout history women have been kept down by the dominant male discourse simply because they were women. The dominant discourse of society — discourse created by powerful men and enforced by both men *and* women — has worked to stop women from making substantial gains throughout history. Following are some examples of different ways in which women who challenged the dominant discourse were kept in line by the dominant discourse both historically and currently.

Witch Trials and Hunts

While the Salem witch trials seem like an exercise in mass hysteria from an easily scared group of people who didn't have an understanding of modern-day science, Karlsen (1998) presents a valid and disturbing view of the trials as a way to punish women for acquiring power or not abiding by society's prescribed sexual order based on gender and biology; Karlsen ties the hysteria to the dominant religion at the time — Puritanism. Nanda and Warms (2009) explain that religion is a powerful social force that can sometimes be a catalyst for change; however it can also have the opposite effect. They add "the function of religion as a force to preserve social order is particularly evident in socially stratified societies, where the elite may invoke religious authority to control the poor" (p. 278). The Salem witch trials show religion being used to keep social stratifications in place, but they also show religion being used by the dominant gender to control the subordinate gender.

The Salem witch trials peaked during Puritanism's peak. "Puritan beliefs were the most powerful determinants of acceptable female behavior, while religious ritual and symbolism continually reinforced behavioral distinctions between the sexes. Gender issues *were* religious issues, and perhaps nowhere is this more vivid than in the case of witchcraft. In Puritan thought, the witch-figure was a symbol of the struggle between God and Satan for human souls. In Puritan society, witches (who as we have seen were usually female) were known by behavior closely or exclusively associated with the female sex" (p. 119). Thus witchcraft was associated with females who were supposedly irrational (female irrationality is a theme we see throughout history and in literature) because they would disrupt the natural, rational order of life, with the natural order being male dominance and female subservience.

However Karlsen goes on to point out that "in their behavior or character, New England witches were in fact not very different from their neighbors…what made witches unusual was not how they behaved but how their behavior was understood in the New England hierarchical society. As older women, in most cases as poor, middling, or unexpectedly well-off women, some of their attributes were construed not simply as unneighborly or sinful — as were similar attitudes and actions in other people — but as evidence of witchcraft, as signs of women's refusal to accept their 'place' in New England's social order." In fact Karlsen found "specific sins of New England witches" included "discontent, anger, envy, malice, seduction, lying, and pride." These were all seen as "offenses against God and the order of creation" (pp. 118 – 119).

What is important to note in the above passage is Karlsen pointing out these women were older and in most cases "poor, middling, or unexpectedly well-off." Older women were those who were approaching or past child bearing years (specifically, they could no longer have a male heir). Poor and middling women were average citizens, and these citizens were traditionally viewed as "less than" the wealthy. The Victorian "sex in brain" argument illustrates how the poor men were not even taken into consideration in their ability to achieve great intelligence because it was assumed they were incapable of this. The unexpectedly well-off women were those who had husbands or male relatives that died and these women became the heirs to substantial male estates. This illustrates that women who could threaten the delicate social order of things were punished by the male discourse, stripping them of any ability they would've had to overcome the dominant discourse's power or even to become part of the dominant discourse. Karlsen does note that as Puritanism and its influence died down, so did the witch trials.

While witch hunts and witch trials are a thing of the past in the United States and in many other countries, they are still happening in remote sections of India whose villages are tribal, poor and, isolated from education and modern health, science, and technology. "Experts say superstitious beliefs are behind some of the attacks, but there are occasions where people — especially widows — are targeted for their land and property" (BBC News, 2014, para. 7). While culture impacts these killings, McCoy (2014) says experts claim these killings are "as much cultural as they are economic and caste-based…Much more often, it isn't superstition but gender and class discrimination. Those accused of sorcery often come from similar backgrounds: female, poor, and of a low caste" (para. 6). Singh claims this is "a legacy of violence against women in our society" and Purwar says, "often a woman is branded a witch so that you can throw her out of the village and grab her land, or to settle scores, family rivalry, or because powerful men want to punish her for spurning their sexual advances. Sometimes, it's used to punish women who question social norms" (as cited in McCoy, 2014, para. 7-8). Women accused of witchcraft in India have been beaten with weapons by fellow villagers, have been beheaded, have been raped, and have endured other forms of torture and death. Groups are working to spread awareness and education. Also, a law that specifically prohibits witch hunting was introduced in April 2015 but, as of the time of publication of this book, was still not passed by the Assam High Court; Assam is an area where these killings are prevalent (Jaiswal, 2015).

Clearly being a woman could, and in some parts of the world still does, bring dangerous consequences. These consequences have been based on cultural beliefs that perpetuate violence against women, particularly against lower class women.

Victorian "Sex in Brain" Debate

The Victorian "sex in brain" debate was discussed in greater detail earlier in this book, but it bears repeating here because it is an important example of ways in which society attempted to deny women the privilege of becoming part of the dominant discourse. This debate linked evolution to cognitive ability and said that since women had smaller brains than men, women were unfit for achieving the same greatness as men. This debate was used as an argument against women obtaining higher education — their biology (and by extension their gender) made them unfit for greatness, so there was no point in them obtaining higher education. The debate drew attention away from intelligence and placed it on biology. Anthropology addresses this type of thinking with its private/public dichotomy theory. "This theory holds that female subordination is based on women's universal role as mothers and homemakers," and societies are divided into a "less prestigious domestic (private) world and a more prestigious (public) world;" women have traditionally inhabited the private world while men have traditionally inhabited the public world. "However, subsequent research revealed that the private/public dichotomy is not universal but rather is most characteristic of the highly gender stratified 19th-century capitalist societies, such as those of Victorian Europe and the United States, where productive relationships moved out of the household and middle-class women (but not working-class women) retreated into the home" (Nanda & Warms, 2009, p. 180).

But women did proceed to higher education, and they proved that a smaller brain size did not equal a lesser ability to think and to achieve. Unfortunately, when society was unable to use brain size as a way to keep women from higher education and possibly changing the dominant discourse's social order, society fell back on gender norms and gender stereotypes to objectify women by drawing attention away from their intelligence and focusing attention on their femininity.

Radcliffe College's Image

The case of Radcliffe College is a perfect example of drawing attention away from intelligence and placing it on femininity. Clemente (2009) explains how students at the all-female Radcliffe College, despite having academic abilities to rival those of students at the neighboring, all-male Harvard College, and administrators at Radcliffe felt the need to recast the school's image to prove women there were not doomed to a life of spinsterhood.

Radcliffe College was one of the prestigious Seven Sisters all-female colleges. These colleges "drew the most vicious condemnations" of critics opposed to women in higher education. "Seven Sisters graduates, with their career ambitions and perceived low marriage rates, were not to be ignored. Not only did they threaten men's livelihoods; they threatened the very existence of the American family" (Clemente, 2009, pp. 638 – 639). Clemente goes on to tell readers, "The basis for the claim that Radcliffe students were unattractive is difficult to establish, but the opinion was widely held and graphic: Radcliffe women had stringy hair and shiny noses; they wore flat shoes, rumpled clothing, and thick glasses. Among the women's most caustic critics were their male neighbors across the Yard, whose publications provided plenty of fodder for periodicals around the country" (p. 639). Being unattractive and having career ambitions carried with it the implication that these women were not marriage material and were thus doomed to a life of spinsterhood which was — and still is — something women are conditioned to fear. Thus society was turning Radcliffe, and by extension high academic achievement and career ambitions of women, into something to be feared and avoided rather than something to be applauded and encouraged. This parallels the old maid librarian stereotype. Career librarians were depicted as unattractive spinsters, while the librarians who gave up their careers for marriage were depicted as pretty; thus career ambitions were to be feared.

Radcliffe and all of the Seven Sisters schools faced criticism for decades about producing future spinsters despite the fact that marriage rates between women at coeducational colleges and women's colleges were roughly equal. "Time and again, administrators had to remind the American public that the Seven Sisters were not a breeding ground for old maids" (Clemente, 2009, p. 644). Clemente tells us as far back as the 1900s, Radcliffe administrators were trying to draw attention to their students' femininity. She then tells us although the American public eventually "warmed to the notion of an educated woman, Americans preferred the lipstick-wielding coed over the frumpily clad 'Cliffie. [Author R. Le Clerc] Phillips carefully distinguished 'the increasing class of girls who merely go to college' from the 'highly intelligent' who attend women's colleges 'for purely intellectual purposes'…The boy-crazy, spend-happy coed was often portrayed as more devoted to fashion than coursework" (p. 646).

Rather than society applauding women who attended college for the sake of academic pursuits, which is the actual point of attending college, society looked down on them because their priorities didn't fit the prescribed social order of the dominant discourse. In order to combat this problem, Radcliffe College created a press board to engage in a modern-day image management campaign. "The educated woman's physical appearance was, time and again, the primary focus of the public's gaze, and the school's publicists did not back away from the responsibility of ensuring that the image was as appealing as it could possibly be. The goal of Radcliffe's publicity department was simple: to encourage the local and national press to portray its students as multifaceted young women who had both brains *and* beauty" (Clemente, 2009, p. 651). Radcliffe students also took the battle personally and "they turned inward, creating a campus culture governed by self-regulation. Applying their own standards to social dictates about femininity, they made and enforced dress codes." They also "diligently documented their popularity with nearby men's colleges" (Clemente, 2009, p. 656). Clearly the women became caught in the self-objectification trap to prove they were attractive in addition to intelligent.

The women also wrote about the men at Harvard in an unflattering way similar to how the men wrote about them. But despite Harvard men's looks being attacked, it was never necessary for them to prove they could be handsome and marriageable as well as highly educated. The men at Harvard College were not subject to the double bind women faced in which they were either smart or attractive, but not both. The men could easily be both or neither without facing criticism.

From 1900 through 1950, Radcliffe students, and no doubt students at other women's colleges, were forced to balance their own ambitions with the expectations society placed on them and prove they were marriage material. They were engaged in a struggle between Mead's aforementioned "I" and "me," — the "I" was the independent woman who cared about her academics more than her looks while the "me" was the woman the public wanted, one who cared more about her looks. This struggle detracted society from their intelligence and instead placed it on their looks. Society was telling them it's not okay for them to just be smart — they must primarily be pretty and secondarily, if at all, be smart. These women were objectified, and they eventually turned to self-objectification. Objectification was society's way of drawing attention away from their abilities, and this took away from their power to enter and challenge the dominant discourse.

Professional Women and Their Objectification in the 21st Century

While it is true that women's colleges no longer need to mount publicity campaigns to prove they don't produce spinsters, and while it's true that society allows women to have careers in addition to marriages and families, society still has not stopped drawing attention to femininity over intelligence. Also, women are often referred to in a diminutive fashion that reduces the respect they should receive. Despite our gains with equality, women must deal with this objectification in the workplace; it's unfortunately blatantly obvious with women in politics and science.

The 2008 presidential primaries were a prime example of this objectification. Senator Hillary Rodham Clinton was a Democratic presidential nominee whose femininity was constantly called into question by the media (yes, by the news media who should've been focused on the facts at hand to help the public determine a competent leader for the country). Clinton's appearance was considered more masculine because she wore pant suits, sensible shoes, light make up, and a simple, short hairstyle. Rather than being happy to have a candidate who could look professional and capable while at the same time looking like she cared more about the country than her wardrobe, she was criticized for not being feminine enough. Her opponent, former Senator and current President Barack Obama, was not criticized for his looks, nor were his looks (other than his African American race) a major focus of the media's attention. Clinton's femininity drew more criticism when Governor Sarah Palin was chosen as presidential candidate Senator John McCain's running mate. Palin was the perfect foil for Clinton's femininity, or perceived lack thereof. Palin wore skirt suits, more make up than Clinton, and her longer hair in an up do. Later, in 2010, as the U.S. Secretary of State, Clinton was asked during an interview in Central Asia's Kyrgyzstan what clothing designer she preferred. Clinton responded with, "Would you ever ask a man that question?" The moderator responded, "Probably not" (Amira, 2010, para. 2). What's troubling isn't just that she was asked this in another country, demonstrating that objectification of women spans cultures, but also that she was asked this just minutes after discussing sexist attitudes toward female lawyers. It was as if her comments about sexism and objectifying women — comments which specifically discussed men's courtroom wardrobe not being a focus of attention like women's courtroom wardrobe is — didn't matter at all.

In addition to focusing on femininity and wardrobe, women in politics are often not referred to in a manner that conveys the same level of respect afforded men. For example, the media frequently referred to Hillary Clinton as Hillary rather than Clinton while Clinton's male colleagues were referred to by their last names. Also, former Secretary of

State Condoleezza Rice was often referred to in the media and in professional situations by her peers as "Condi." Other members of President George W. Bush's cabinet were never referred to in a diminutive fashion like this; for example, Donald Rumsfeld was never referred to as "Donnie" in professional communications or in the media.

More recently, in 2015, Sir Tim Hunt, a Nobel Prize winner and a Royal Society Fellow, was sharply criticized for his remarks about women working in science laboratories. BBC News (2015) reported Hunt made the following remarks during a conference in South Korea: "Let me tell you about the trouble with girls. Three things happen when they are in the lab: you fall in love with them, they fall in love with you, and when you criticise them they cry" (para. 6-7). Hunt later told the media he meant this as a "light-hearted, ironic comment," but it also had some honesty (BBC News, 2015, para. 10). Hunt admitted "I have fallen in love with people in the lab and people in the lab have fallen in love with me and it's very disruptive to the science because it's terribly important that in a lab people are on a level playing field" (BBC News, 2015, para. 13). Hunt referred to women as girls, thus diminishing their professional respect. He also neglected to accept any part of the blame or responsibility for falling in love and creating this distracting atmosphere, as if he was tricked into falling in love by a manipulative girl. Part of the criticism Hunt drew for his statement came in the form of female scientists and their male supporters from across the globe who took to Twitter and tweeted photos of female scientists at work doing dirty jobs in unattractive biohazard gear or tweeted photos of signs in their lab that jokingly prohibited falling in love. The tweets included the hashtag #DistractinglySexy. Backlash against Hunt's comments followed by a reverse discourse twitter campaign by both women and men shows promise that the view of women in sciences is improving; however this reaction was to overtly sexist comments. More covert forms of sexism in the workplace still exist and are often ignored or taken for granted as the norm. This must be changed in order for women to truly gain workplace equality.

Bringing the conversation back around to libraries, we can see that stereotypes adjusted to focus on femininity when scare tactics of spinsterhood no longer applied. The old maid was the dominant stereotype for most of the profession's history, and we still see it lingering in the background; but the sexy librarian has emerged as a stereotype that is replacing the old maid. Both stereotypes focus on looks as opposed to skills and abilities, and neither stereotype has a male librarian equivalent. Once society could no longer use the old maid stereotype as a cautionary tale for women who had career ambitions, society turned to objectification. It is true that librarians may have played a role in perpetuating this sexy librarian stereotype because they wanted to shed the old maid stereotype, but society's love of objectifying women to keep them in their gender norm place will ensure this stereotype's persistence.

Society has a dangerous history of brining the focus of women back to their femininity, whether that focus is used to keep women from obtaining wealth, education, a career, or even true equality. Thus the stereotype of the sexy librarian may never go away. In fact if Roberto's (2014) future scenario comes true and we are all either CIOs or archivists, you can bet unless society's reaction to women gaining a foothold on the dominant discourse changes that we will have sexy CIO and sexy archivist stereotypes.

What Can We Do?

With all of these cultural, linguistic, and psychosocial forces pulling us in different directions and impacting the ability to change stereotypes, fighting and changing stereotypes is an uphill battle. It's possible to disprove stereotypes reactively, but it is time to be proactive and show who librarians are rather than letting the media tell us who we are; after all, Keer and Carlos (2014) tell us "as a group, librarians have historically allowed others to define their image and their self-worth…By allowing outside media and outside scholars to define who we are as a profession, we lose agency in creating our images and, to a greater extent, the stereotypes that arise about our profession" ("Negotiations of Class," para. 13). Replacing one stereotype with another is not going to change anything; then again, setting out to change stereotypes that are ingrained in our culture because they're created by our language and our views on gender is a daunting and maybe impossible goal to tackle in a lifetime. The following steps are steps any librarian can take to change the professional and cultural tide on concrete and more abstract levels; while these steps are listed separately, they overlap in theory and in practice. It's important to remember that some cultural shifts make take decades to occur, and we must not get discouraged by what seems like an uphill battle that is not showing the results we would like. A concerted and sustained effort must be made to get forces moving in the direction of change.

Discover a shared identity and a common brand for the profession.

This is something librarians must do if we ever expect to overcome stereotypes. One of the survey respondents from this book's study pointed out this need that also shows up in the literature: "Librarians seem to lack much of a self-identity." This lack of self-identity is one of the reasons stereotypes remain prevalent — without it there is no clear understanding of what librarians do or the required education to do it, and people fall back on stereotypes to fill in the knowledge gaps. Determining the shared identity and shared vision of the profession will not be easy because the profession is so varied; however, there are common beliefs and values that are held by all fields of librarianship that can be used as a starting point for this shared identity and vision.

Overcome internal divisions.

In order to truly change the public's view of the profession, we must start internally; after all, as Roberto (2014) says, "We can and will worry about externally projected stereotypes of library workers all we'd like, but the ones we project on each other are ultimately most concerning" (para. 1). Some librarians who do not embody the stereotype may think those whose personality naturally exudes some of the stereotypical qualities (i.e. wearing comfy shoes, having an affinity for books, being quiet and reserved) are hurting the profession and the less stereotypical librarians may pressure (or even bully) the others into denying these aspects of their personalities; the reverse is also true and more conservative librarians may pressure or bully less conservative librarians into becoming more stereotypically conservative.

Another internal division that can cause friction is a lack of consistency regarding credentials for entry into the profession. It's no wonder patrons have a fuzzy idea of the education required to be a librarian when some librarian jobs require master's degrees or bachelor's degrees in library science while others only require some library experience or related experience or only library coursework. There are also many librarian jobs whose titles do not contain the word "librarian," so patrons can't always guess at the required education either. This inconsistency in education and job title is why the researcher of this book's survey did not limit her research to participants who had specific degrees or whose titles were "librarian." These inconsistencies sometimes lead to differences in who we consider "real" librarians and this could lead us to pressure or bully those without library science master's degrees from ALA-accredited universities (the profession's "gold standard" of library education) to obtain these degrees when they are not required. This pressure and bullying could also lead potentially valuable colleagues to leave the profession. This division and resulting pressure was alluded to in a survey response when participants were asked, "How do you think stereotypes impact people's desire to become a librarian?": "I can only speak from personal experience…I have tossed around the possibility of returning to school to receive my M.L.S. Now, it's more like I want to return to school to get some additional experience to enhance my existing educational background. Obtaining an M.L.S. may not guarantee acceptance in the field when there are other contributing factors (that cannot be changed) that serve as obstacles."

Finally, we must end the internal divisions over the value of big and small librarianship; this ties into the division over credentials and education. Big librarianship is typically viewed as more prestigious because of the advanced degrees required and the employment at universities and major research institutions. Small librarianship is typically viewed as less prestigious — it doesn't require a multitude of advanced degrees (and may not require any advanced degree), and it often entails work in school libraries and in small public libraries in underserved communities. While working for a major research institution and achieving goals on a global scale may seem like more important work than work done by a librarian who works with patrons that struggle to read, in reality both jobs are just as important and are required for communities to grow. Basic literacy skills are also the building blocks that enable people to make achievements on a global scale. We are culturally inclined to view large-scale achievements as more prestigious than small-scale achievements. We are also culturally inclined to value the work of men more than the work of women, and big librarianship has traditionally been the realm of men while small librarianship has traditionally been the realm of women. The value we place on big and small librarianship achievements must change. As a profession, we must value all achievements of all libraries and librarians.

Clearly these internal divisions must receive as much attention as external stereotypes receive, and these divisions must be overcome. If we can't value different areas of our profession, we can't expect the public to value them.

Think like a public relations manager.

The present study and the literature reveal the need for better assessment of library outreach and marketing efforts; after all, if we still think our public has stereotypical views of the profession after decades of trying to fight stereotypes, then our efforts to combat those stereotypes have not been successful. Perhaps what we have been doing — or haven't been doing — is part of the problem. Many librarians have social media sites that are the opposite of one stereotype but are the embodiment of another; is that actually helping our image? Are calendars with tattooed and cat loving librarians helping our image? Is community programming adding to the value of the library or is it taking away some of its value (i.e. there is often debate about whether having video games in the library turns the children's area into a television babysitter)? Are our information literacy efforts being assessed to show how we are positively impacting our students, or are we letting university and school administrators think the concepts we teach can be taught by English teachers and our resources can be provided by Google? Thinking like a public relations manager and strategically planning initiatives and services, marketing them, and then critically assessing our initiatives is necessary; this will allow us to focus our limited time and resources on programs and services that will benefit our patrons and our professional image. More librarians must be cognizant of the necessity to engage in this strategic planning and assessment.

Assess and improve library education

Library education programs should also be preparing future librarians to meet the ever-changing demands of the profession. Competent, professional graduates who possess technology, outreach, and teaching skills in addition to traditional library science skills are necessary, yet some or all of these areas are often overlooked in programs.

Library instruction, management, and interpersonal and business communication do appear in library school curricula, but they are often electives as opposed to core courses; library school programs should include some kind of a business core so everyone graduates with at least a basic understanding of these concepts. Brecher and Klipfel (2014) discuss the need for education training for academic librarians now that information literacy instruction is one of their primary responsibilities: "A background in pedagogy is particularly important for these librarians, who are increasingly expected to collaborate on equal terms with faculty in teaching information literacy and critical thinking skills. A background in theory and psychology can situate the librarian as an equal in relationships with other faculty and can allow the librarian to be a major contributor to the partnership" (p. 44). The need for business and communication skills was reflected in a respondent's short answer response on the survey: "Library schools have to devote more instruction towards business and communication skills so librarians can be better managers and accepted as peers by other professionals."

Roemer (2015) tells readers LIS students whose goal is to work in academic lack training in measuring scholarship impact despite the fact that this measurement is necessary in academic. She suggests that, in addition to learning about traditional measures of scholarship, these LIS students learn about altmetrics (metrics based on social media and other Internet outlets) to measure the impact of scholarship: "The subject of scholarship — a key requirement of many academic librarian positions — remains relatively neglected by LIS programs across the country. Newly hired librarians are often surprised by the realities of their long term performance expectations, and can especially struggle to find evidence of their impact on the larger LIS profession or field of research over time" (para. 2). Roemer adds altmetrics "open up the door to researchers who…are engaged in online spaces and networks that include members beyond the academy" ("What is Altmetrics?," para. 2).

Our peers, both librarians and colleagues in other fields we work with, must respect us or the working relationship will not be viewed as a relationship of equals. In order improve library education, programs must be assessed; follow ups should be done with graduates at specific intervals post-graduation, and employers should be interviewed to determine the types of skills needed in the profession and whether or not they believe the program provided these skills. These follow ups will also allow program administrators to see identify changing trends in the field and to be proactive about adjusting the curriculum rather than reactive and adjusting it after graduates who are not properly prepared have entered the workforce.

Demonstrate your skills and abilities, but don't be a "know it all"

We must engage with our community — whether our community is a campus, a municipality, or a business — in ways that let our community learn about us and see what we are capable of doing. Pho and Masland (2014) tell us, and as other literature and this survey's responses indicate, "The public does not know what librarians do, which produces misconceptions about our professional image" (para. 4). Literature and survey results also show that the public doesn't have a clear understanding of the education required to become a librarian. The field of library outreach emerged to market library services; despite increased marketing of library services, we have seen that stereotypes related to our skills and abilities still abound. Thus in addition to marketing we must, as survey respondents pointed out, be adaptable (i.e. we must be ready to learn new things and adjust services as needed), and we must also demonstrate our skills and abilities. Librarians often come to the field with a variety of skills and abilities that extend far beyond the librarianship realm. Lowe-Wincentsen (2011) says that a fall 2009 survey about librarian career choices revealed only 25% of respondents chose librarianship as a first career; past fields included "publishing, legal, retail, or IT" (pp. 100 – 102). In addition to past careers, some fields of librarianship require continuing education beyond a degree in library science. Clearly librarians are educated and skilled people with varied backgrounds and we shouldn't be modest, but we also shouldn't be smug, about what we can offer patrons and our larger communities.

We must interact with people both inside and outside of our library; in fact there may be times when we can only demonstrate the full range of our skills and abilities by going outside of the library and getting involved in other parts of our community that allow us to do other types of work or take part in activities we enjoy. For example, if you enjoy gaming then get involved with gaming groups on campus. If you have an accounting background, volunteer to assist people with taxes. If you enjoy local politics, take part in municipal council meetings; this is also a great way to keep your municipal government aware of the library and its needs and services. Kranich and Lotts (2015) stressed the importance of this "turning outward" in a presentation in which Kranich told attendees we cannot afford to have an "edifice complex" and stay hidden in our buildings. Kranich urges us to get out in our communities and "build connections, not collections."

Being engaged with and involved in the community also allows the public to see librarians outside the library setting so they learn a bit more about their personalities and abilities; the public will feel more comfortable approaching someone it knows, and it will also see the whole person and realize individual librarians are not stereotypes. Community involvement has the added benefit of attracting more attention and support for your library.

Be visible in your library

In addition to turning outward and being engaged with your community, you must be visible in your library. It's easy to get stuck in your office for weeks at a time when you're doing behind the scenes work; this happens too often and patrons only interact with paraprofessionals, which contributes to their notions that anyone who works in a library is a librarian and that librarians only shelve books and do clerical tasks. Get out from behind your desk or get out of your office and interact with patrons. Some libraries have implemented a roving reference service model where they take their mobile devices to other parts of the library, or even to other parts of campus if it's an academic library, to assist patrons where they are working rather than waiting for patrons to come to the library; while this hasn't been successful in all libraries, you must determine what your patrons respond to best. We can't always wait for patrons to come to us; patrons may be shy, they may not want to lose their seat in the library (especially if their seat is one of the few places with an easily accessible electrical outlet or if they are using a computer when computers are in high demand), and they may think they are bothering you if they see you working on something else and they "interrupt" you. Finally, patrons may not realize they have a problem or that help for their problem is easily accessible until they see a librarian.

If it's not possible to implement roving reference services, something as simple as a "Get to Know Your Librarians" poster hanging up in the library or section of a library newsletter that features a different librarian in each issue will work. Make sure the information presents you as a professional and mentions your education but also shows you as an approachable, down to earth person who is more than happy to work with patrons.

Engage in professional development

Weingand told readers in 1999, "the shelf life of a degree is approximately three years and declining. Maintaining competence and learning new skills must be at the top of every professional's 'To Do' list. It is an ethical responsibility, to be sure, but also one that is pragmatic and critical for career success…Continuing professional education is no longer an option, it is a requirement of professional practice (p. 201)" (as cited in Cooke, 2011, p. 2). This was true more than 15 years ago, and with the rapid advances in technology and information science a degree's shelf life may be even shorter now. In addition to Weingand explaining the importance of professional development for careers, he states it is an "ethical responsibility." This is a different approach to professional development than the literature and survey responses have touched on, but it is clear to see why librarians should view professional development as an ethical responsibility of the profession. Librarians have a duty to provide their patrons with appropriate resources and services and, as the tide shifts from librarians being the gatekeepers of resources to librarians guiding people on correct use of resources, it is even more critical for librarians to engage in professional development to understand what resources are out there and how people interact with those resources. If librarians don't understand their users and don't provide resources to meet their needs, libraries will not serve their purposes. Engaging in professional development is also necessary for the life of the profession; librarians who don't engage in professional development and who don't stay abreast of the changing needs of patrons are allowing people to believe their libraries are irrelevant and possibly useless in today's society. "By not proactively seeking continuing education, librarians are 'not actively pursuing obsolescence, but there are indications that some are passively permitting it to overtake them'" (Stone, 1971, p. 436, as cited in Cooke, 2011, p. 2).

      Professional development comes in many forms (i.e. conferences, courses, etc.) and may be called many different names (i.e. continuing education), thus "it's very important for the individual librarian to 'be on the same page' as their supervisor or evaluator in terms of just what constitutes such development" (LaGuardia, 2014, para. 2). It is also important to keep in mind that library science is both a social science and an information science field, and the type of professional development may be impacted by the field of librarianship you work in. Honing your communication skills or learning more about user groups and search habits are necessary for the social science aspect of the profession while keeping abreast of technology advances is necessary for the information science aspect of the profession. We also cannot forget that library science has heavy components from the education field. Librarians who engage in information literacy should take advantage of professional development to learn about pedagogical and androgogical theories and techniques. Also, if you work in a specialized field or if you liaise with specialized departments, it would be beneficial to engage in corresponding professional development to be able to understand and communicate the discipline's concepts and be seen as a peer. For example, librarians who work in health sciences should learn about healthcare informatics to see how library resources contribute to that field. And librarians who engage in outreach should attend public relations and marketing webinars or conferences to get a broader view of their work. Looking at your profession through a subject-specific lens as opposed to a field-specific lens can help you think outside the library box.

Utilize technology, but don't ignore print.

While it's true that library users overwhelmingly prefer electronic access to print, and while it's true that library users may be technophiles, we can't ignore print when that is the best resource or most financially feasible option. We certainly can't ignore print because we think patrons will perceive us as old-fashioned. And while keeping abreast of new technology and offering patrons the technology they want is necessary, we can't jump on the technology bandwagon and devote all of our budgets to purchasing the latest and greatest technology just to have it nor should we strive to become bookless libraries. Libraries mean different things to different people, and you must balance those expectations in your collections. It's also foolish to fall into the "everything is available electronically" trap — our profession knows better than that, yet it is still easy for us to fall into that trap when we are trying to get patrons to use our services. We can't forget that while electronic formats work well for some resources, they don't work well for others; for example, graphics may appear better in print than onscreen, so a print book may be best for an art history course. Also we must take into account usage issues associated with electronic formats such as e-books, including simultaneous access, devices required to access the material, and device maintenance. Licensing and bundle options offered by publishers may not be cost effective, so that is another reason a print item may be best for your library. Don't shy away from recommending a print resource when it's the best resource for a patron's needs. If the patron is upset or inquisitive about having to use print, briefly explain your reasons for having the item in print. Explaining decisions related to cost and use in terms patrons will understand (not in library lingo will) help your patrons better understand the library and it will not leave a "knowledge gap" that must be filled with the stereotype of librarians only working with and understanding print.

Be adaptable.

Ranganathan's fifth law of librarianship tells us "the library is a growing organism" (USC Marshall, 2015). The community in which the library is situated is also a growing organism; thus as the community grows and changes, the library must grow and change with it. The library should also work to facilitate some of the changes a community faces; for example, as the world increasingly moves toward digital communication as the primary means of communication, libraries can help bridge the digital divide by providing access to computers and providing training on how to use computer programs so the community members can keep pace with the world.

The main components of the library profession are also changing and we must adapt to these changes. Technology is constantly changing, and this impacts what our patrons expect of us and what services we can and should — or should not — provide. Technology also fails, so we must be prepared to provide services without it. The trade and scholarly publishing landscapes are changing, and this impacts how we can develop our collections and how patrons can utilize our collection. The face of education is changing, and this will impact how we deliver information literacy sessions and how we are integrated in school and college curricula. Clearly librarians must be willing and ready to adapt to these changes and their results if we want to serve our communities and stay relevant.

Gear programming to the needs of your community, even if those needs don't relate to library services and resources.

Libraries can be valuable to the community even when the community is not using the library for resources but just for space. Do community groups need places to meet? Do students from local school districts need places to offer after-school tutoring? The library can provide the space for these services, and that will at least get people through the library doors. The intent of people coming into the library may not be to use the library, but as they are coming into the library and waiting for their meetings to begin, they will take notice of what the library offers. The library should also serve as a place for information, even if the information is coming from a discussion as opposed to library resources. For example, if your community members are worried about a recent health scare or if they are interested in what is happening politically in certain areas of the world, invite local experts to host discussions on these issues in the library. You can then have a display of your resources related to the issues to remind people that they can come to the library to find answers to their questions. Libraries can also team up with local businesses to provide information the community is in need of; for example, if you are an academic library you can team up with your college's financial aid department to host sessions about managing student loan debt or you can team up with your college's career services department for sessions on careers and majors. Libraries must form partnerships to help people see that libraries aren't just places for checking out books. Librarians shouldn't be afraid to have events in the library in which the focus is not on library resources; getting people into the door of the library is a step in the right direction toward getting them to know you exist and have resources. Forming partnerships also lets people see you as an active part of the community.

Be cognizant of society's gender norms and stereotypes, and don't perpetuate them.

Fighting for gender equality is a battle that happens on all fronts, and we must realize that our culture has instilled in us certain predisposed ideas about genders and what they can and can't do. This is reflected in our language, in the visual cues the world provides us, and even in our hiring practices; thus library administrators must be cognizant of these cultural norms and the biases they create and they must work to overcome these biases. For example, when you evaluate a male candidate for a children's librarian position, are you evaluating him based on his skills, or is his gender coloring your opinion? Is this "not a man's job" and so he won't be the right fit? The same is true for promoting someone to administrative positions. Are you choosing to promote men so they end up in positions that are stereotypically more appropriate for men and keeping women in the reference librarian positions because public service jobs are stereotypically more appropriate for women?

Avoid "talking down" about librarianship and genders.

Anecdotally, this book's author has noticed that while public librarians are not shy about their importance, other librarians sometimes feel inferior to their peers who have more prestigious degrees and job titles. This inferiority complex leads them to "talk down," or diminish the importance of, their roles. For example, librarians at academic libraries have said they "only have a master's degree" as opposed to a doctoral degree while librarians working on interdisciplinary health sciences teams have identified themselves as "just a librarian" as opposed to a nurse or a physician. Librarians shouldn't be modest about their degrees or their job titles; people with more prestigious degrees and job titles come to librarians for research assistance, so the services offered by librarians are valuable and necessary components of the work of our peers. We must avoid talking down about ourselves because, if we don't value ourselves and our profession, why should others value us and our profession?

Society also has a tendency to talk down about men and women depending on the scenario. Men's ability to do domestic chores is often mocked while a female's inability to do something may be attributed to the fact that she's "just a girl." Engaging in this kind of judgment makes it seem like these faults are inherent aspects of their genders. While avoiding talking down about genders will not single-handedly change our culture's views on gender, we must be examples in our quest to change the tide of how society views genders and the resultant unequal treatment of genders.

Seek diversity in your staff and in your collections.

Pho and Masland (2014) point out the need to diversify the field so people can see librarians who span the age, gender, race/ethnicity, and sexual orientation spectrum. When patrons see a variety of people doing library jobs, this shows them that anyone who is capable of handling the job and educational requirements can enter the profession. It is important to choose candidates who are qualified above any other characteristic, which is why we must also encourage diversity in library education in order to have a diverse pool of qualified applicants. In addition to a diversified workforce, librarians should develop their collections with materials that show a wide variety of people doing a wide variety of tasks; for example, a children's librarian should choose books that show male and female librarians of different ages and ethnicities and should also choose books that show boys and girls taking part in activities that cross traditional gender boundaries. These actions will help combat the aforementioned misinformation effect in which exposure to the wrong information (particularly to stereotypical views that are incorrect) can lead us to misremember things; as we remember, we feel in memory gaps with plausible guesses. Constant exposure to stereotypes provides us with incorrect information about a gender, profession, etc., yet those exposures seem credible because we have seen them so many times. Thus we fall back on these stereotypical representations to fill in our memory gaps.

Don't replace one stereotype with another.

Replacing one stereotype with another may demonstrate who you are not, but it doesn't demonstrate who you are. Librarians attempted to shed the old maid stereotype, but in doing so a plethora of other stereotypes have grown up around us, and they come with both positive and negative connotations. We must avoid falling into the trap Roberto (2014) described that was discussed earlier in this chapter — the trap of becoming either IT people because of our rampant technophilia or archivists because of our nostalgia for the past — and just be ourselves. If we enjoy some of the stereotypical qualities of librarianship, then we should not deny that aspect of ourselves. We must also not turn down a potential librarian candidate who looks like the stereotypical librarian; in fact Pagowsky and Rigby (2014) tell us, "we also need to be careful of excluding by force those who do fit the stereotype" (para. 41). Is a candidate being turned down because he or she is naturally quiet and conservative and enjoys books? Forcing out one stereotype and replacing it with the "anti-stereotype" means the anti-stereotype will become the new stereotype once the profession is flooded with these images.

Rather than attempting to replace one stereotype with another, we must be professional and pleasant in actions and appearance because this professionalism will leave a lasting impression on everyone, even on those patrons whose questions didn't require a major demonstration of our skills and even on those patrons who may have been hesitant to use the library and approach librarians. After all, as one survey respondent said, "The general public doesn't really understand all that a librarian does in their job, but if we are pleasant and helpful I think we will be appreciated and the profession will be admired."

Remember the rules.

Sometimes the best thing to do to think about how to advance the profession or how to improve images of the profession is to go back to the basic rules; unfortunately this is another concept that is missing from many LIS programs, so many new graduates don't know about the rules. Dr. S. R. Ranganathan developed five rules, or laws, of librarianship in 1931, and these laws are still applicable to the profession:

1. "Books are for use."
2. "Every book its reader."
3. "Every reader his book."
4. "Save the time of the reader."
5. "The library is a growing organism" (USC Marshall, 2015).

Applying these laws to librarianship today, you have:
1. Build collections that will be useful to your patrons.
2. There are readers for each type of book.
3. Seek diversity in your collection because just as different books attract different types of readers, different readers enjoy different books. Your library services and resources must serve all of your patrons, not just a small group of patrons.
4. We must make our collections accessible so patrons can quickly and easily find what they need. We want patrons to spend time using our resources, not searching for them.
5. Librarians must be adaptable so our libraries can grow and change as our communities grown and change.

In 1998, during his American Library Association presidency, Michael Gorman used Ranganathan's rules as a base to create five new rules of librarianship. These rules are rather straightforward in relation to librarianship today, and their essence has come up throughout the literature and survey results in this book; thus these rules must also be heeded:
1. "Libraries serve humanity."
2. "Respect all forms by which knowledge is communicated."
3. "Use technology intelligently to enhance service."
4. "Protect free access to knowledge."
5. "Honor the past and create the future" (USC Marshall, 2015).

Conclusion

Clearly there are many things librarians can do professionally to change stereotypes; however this is also a cultural battle we must fight on all fronts. We must fight for equality for everyone, and we must be cognizant of the latent biases and stereotypes in our language. We must also strive to let the world exist in grays as opposed to black and white dichotomies, and we must encourage women to stop self-objectifying. All of these actions done in combination with the professional steps we must take will help change the cultural tide of stereotypes; it may take generations to see all of these changes, but libraries must take advantage of the historical spot they are in now — gender and other professional issues are at the forefront of politics, the world is becoming predominantly digital, and we have a generation whose only frame of reference is a digital age. Libraries and librarians are at a pivotal moment in time, and this moment can help the profession or hurt the profession depending on what we choose to do about stereotypes. Now is the time for librarians to be activists for themselves in addition to being activists for their communities.

References and Bibliography

Adams, K. C. (2000). Loveless frump as hip and sexy party girl: A reevaluation of the old-maid stereotype. *The Library Quarterly, 70*(3), 287–301.

A "librarian" in song. (2008). *Library Journal, 133*(11), 15.

Amira, D. (2010, December 2). Hillary Clinton is asked what designers she wears moments after making point about sexism. Retrieved from http://nymag.com/daily/intelligencer/2010/12/hillary_clinton_asked_what_des.html

Andersen, M. L. (1988). *Thinking about women: Sociological perspectives on sex and gender* (2nd ed.). New York: Macmillan Publishing Company.

Archer, E. M. (2012). The power of gendered stereotypes in the US Marine Corps. *Armed Forces & Society, 39*(2), 359–391. doi:10.1177/0095327X12446924

Association of College and Research Libraries. (2015). *Academic library contributions to student success: Documented practices from the field.* Chicago: Association of College and Research Libraries.

Attebury, R. I. (2010). Perceptions of a profession: Librarians and stereotypes in online videos. *Library Philosophy and Practice*, 1–22.

BBC News (2014, October 27). India woman killed in 'witch hunts.' *BBC.com.* Retrieved from http://www.bbc.com/news/world-asia-india-29782808

BBC News (2015, June 11). Sir Tim Hunt resigns from university role over girls comment. *BBC.com.* Retrieved from http://www.bbc.com/news/uk-33090022

Battles, M. (2003). *Library: An unquiet history.* New York: W.W. Norton & Company.

Bennett, A. & Royle, N. (2004). *An introduction to literature, criticism, and theory* (3rd ed.). New York: Pearson.

Bobbit-Zeher, D. (2011). Gender discrimination at work: Connecting gender stereotypes, institutional policies, and gender composition of workplace. *Gender & Society, 25*(6), 764–786. doi:10.1177/0891243211424741

Boddice, R. (2011). The manly mind? Revisiting the Victorian "sex in brain" debate. *Gender & History, 23*(2), 321–340.

Borrelli, C. (2013, July 2). Hipsters, librarians check each other out: At meeting, tradition, future on same page. *Chicago Tribune.*

Brannon, L. (2005). *Gender: Psychological perspectives* (4th ed.). New York: Pearson.

Brecher, D., & Klipfel, K.M. (2014). Education training for instruction librarians: A shared perspective. *Communications in Information Literacy, 8*(1), 43-49. Retrieved from http://tinyurl.com/ntwzosn

Brinkerhoff, D.B., White, L.K., Ortega, S.K., & Weitz, R. (2008). *Essentials of psychology* (7th ed.). Belmont, CA: Thomson Wadsworth.

Burns, G. (1998). *Librarians in fiction: A critical bibliography*. Jefferson, North Carolina: McFarland & Company.

Burns, N., & Grove, S. K. (2009). *The practice of nursing research: Appraisal, synthesis, and generation of evidence* (6th ed.). St. Louis, MO: Saunders.

Chiang, H. H. (2010). Liberating sex, knowing desire: Scientia sexualis and epistemic turning points in the history of sexuality. *History of the Human Sciences, 23*(5), 42–69. doi:10.1177/0952695110378947

Church, G. M. (2002). In the eye of the beholder: How librarians have been viewed over time. In Wendi Arrant & Candace R. Benefiel (Eds.), *The image and role of the librarian* (pp. 5–24). Binghamton, New York: The Haworth Information Press.

Clemente, D. (2009). "Prettier than they used to be": Femininity, fashion, and the recasting of Radcliffe's reputation, 1900-1950. *The New England Quarterly, LXXXII*(4), 637–666.

Clemons, J. (2011). Leading the way into the future of libraries. In Martin K. Wallace, Rebecca Tolley-Stokes, & Erik Sean Estep (Eds.), *The Generation X librarian: Essays on leadership, technology, pop culture, social responsibility, and professional identity* (pp. 91–98). Jefferson, North Carolina: McFarland & Company.

Cockroft, S., & Rouse, A. (2015, June 9). 'Just look at that monstrous seductress Marie Curie ruining everything': Nobel Prize winner is mocked online for saying women should be banned from male labs. *Daily Mail*. Retrieved from http://www.dailymail.co.uk/news/article-3117648/Ban-women-male-labs-distracting-cry-criticised-says-Nobel-prize-winner-Sir-Tim-Hunt.html

Cooke, N.A. (2011, August). *Professional development 2.0 for librarians: Developing an online personal learning network (PLN)*. Paper presented at the conference of The International Federation of Library Associations and Institutions, Puerto Rico. Retrieved from http://conference.ifla.org/ifla77

Cullen, J. (2000, May). On my mind: Rupert Giles, the professional-image slayer. *American Libraries, 31*(5), 42.

Culler, J. (1997). *Literary theory: A very short introduction.* Oxford: Oxford University Press.

DeCandido, G. A. (1999, September). Bibliographic good vs. evil in Buffy the Vampire Slayer. *American Libraries, 30*(8), 44–47.

Dickinson, T. E. (2002). Looking at the male librarian stereotype. In Wendi Arrant & Candace R. Benefiel (Eds.), *The image and role of the librarian* (pp. 97–110). Binghamton, New York: The Haworth Information Press.

Dilevko, J., & Gottlieb, L. (2004). The portrayals of librarians in obituaries at the end of the twentieth century. *The Library Quarterly, 74*(2), 152–180.

Fagan, J. (2002). Students' perceptions of academic librarians. In Wendi Arrant & Candace R. Benefiel (Eds.), *The image of role of the librarian* (pp. 131–148). Binghamton, New York: The Haworth Information Press.

Fain, J. A. (2009). *Reading, understanding, and applying nursing research* (3rd ed.). Philadelphia: F.A. Davis.

Ferrier, M. (2014, June 21). The end of the hipster: How flat caps and beards stopped being so cool. *The Guardian.* Retrieved from http://www.theguardian.com/fashion/2014/jun/22/end-of-the-hipster-flat-caps-and-beards

Freeman, M., & Vasconcelos, E. F. S. (2010). Critical social theory: Core tenets, inherent issues. *New Directions for Evaluation, 127,* 7–19. doi:10.1002/ev.335

Gaines, A. (2014). That's women's work: Pink-collar professions, gender, and the librarian stereotype. In Nicole Pagowsky & Miriam Rigby (Eds.), *The librarian stereotype: Deconstructing perceptions & presentations of information work.* Chicago: Association of College & Research Libraries.

Gamson, W. A., Croteau, D., Hoynes, W., & Sasson, T. (1992). Media images and the social construction of reality. *Annual Review of Sociology, 18,* 373–393.

Geeraert, N. (2013). When suppressing one stereotype leads to rebound of another: On the procedural nature of stereotype rebound. *Personality and Social Psychology Bulletin, 39*(9), 1173–1183. doi:10.1177/0146167213493121

Grabe, M. E., & Samson, L. (2011). Sexual cues emanating from the anchorette chair: Implications for perceived professionalism, fitness for beat, and memory for news. *Communication Research, 38*(4), 471–496. doi:10.1177/0093650210384986

Gray, S.W. (2012). Locating librarianship's identity in its historical roots of professional philosophies: Towards a radical new identity for librarians of today (and tomorrow). *International Federation of Library Associations and Institutions, 39*(1), 37-44.

Green, A. I. (2010). Remembering Foucault: Queer theory and disciplinary power. *Sexualities, 13*(3), 316–337. doi:10.1177/1363460709364321

Griffin, E. (2006). *A first look at communication theory* (6th ed.). New York: McGraw-Hill Companies.

Groves, C., & Black, W. (2011). Understanding Gen X at work: Securing the library's future. In Martin K. Wallace, Rebecca Tolley-Stokes, & Erik Sean Estep (Eds.), *The Generation X librarian: Essays on leadership, technology, pop culture, social responsibility, and professional identity* (pp. 18–28). Jefferson, North Carolina: McFarland & Company.

Grubb, M. V., & Billiot, T. (2010). Women sportscasters: Navigating a masculine domain. *Journal of Gender Studies, 19*(1), 87–93. doi:10.1080/09589230903525460

Gunther, C., Ekinci, N. A., Schwieren, C., & Strobel, M. (2010). Women can't jump?-An experiment on competitive attitudes and stereotype threat. *Journal of Economic Behavior & Organization, 75*, 395–401. doi:10.1016/j.jebo.2010.05.003

Hildenbrand, S. (2000). Library feminism and library women's history: Activism and scholarship, equity, and culture. *Libraries & Culture, 35*(1), 51–65.

Hornsey, M. J. (2008). Social identity theory and self-categorization theory: A historical review. *Social and Personality Psychology Compass, 2*(1), 204–222. doi:10.1111/j.1751-9004.2007.00066.x

Jaiswal, N. (2015, July 30). Why witches are still being beheaded in India. *USA Today*. Retrieved from http://usatoday.com/story/news/world/2015/07/29/globalpost-why-witches-still-being-beheaded-india/30827059

Jesella, K. (2007, July 8). A hipper crowd of shushers. *The New York Times*. Retrieved from http://www.nytimes.com/2007/07/08/fashion/08librarian.html?pagewanted=all&_r=0

Johnson, V., & Gurung, R. A. R. (2011). Defusing the objectification of women by other women: The role of competence. *Sex Roles, 65*, 177–188. doi:10.1007/s11199-011-0006-5

Karlsen, C. F. (1998). *The devil in the shape of a woman: Withcraft in Colonial New England*. New York: W.W. Norton & Company.

Keer, G., & Carlos, A. (2014). The stereotype stereotype: Our obsession with librarian representation. In Nicole Pagowsky & Miriam Rigby (Eds.), *The librarian stereotype: Deconstructing perceptions & presentations of information work*. Chicago: Association of College & Research Libraries.

Kenney, B. (2013, May 3). So you think you want to be a librarian? Retrieved from http://www.publishersweekly.com/pw/by-topic/industry-news/libraries/article/57090-so-you-think-you-want-to-be-a-librarian.html

King, S. (1990). The library policeman. In *Four past midnight* (1st ed.). New York: Viking.

Kneale, R. (2009). *You don't look like a librarian: Shattering stereotypes and creating positive new images in the Internet Age*. Medford, New Jersey: Information Today.

Kniffel, L. (2005, January). What we can learn from junk TV - And vice versa. *American Libraries, 36*(1), 44.

Krieglmeyer, R., & Sherman, J. W. (2012). Disentangling stereotype activation and stereotype application in the stereotype misperception task. *Journal of Personality and Social Psychology*, 1–20. doi:10.1037/a0028764

Kranich, N., & Lotts, M. (2015, May). *Listening to many voices: Community conversations at Rutgers University Libraries*. Presentation at the Pennsylvania Library Association College & Research Division workshop, Millersville University of Pennsylvania.

LaGuardia, C. (2014, March). Professional development: What's it to you? *Library Journal*. Retrieved from lj.libraryjournal.com/2014/03/opinion/not-dead-yet/professional-development-whats-it-to-you-not-dead-yet

Landridge, M., Riggi, C., & Schultz, A. (2014). Student perceptions of academic librarians: The influence of pop culture and past experience. In Nicole Pagowsky & Miriam Rigby (Eds.), *The librarian stereotype: Deconstructing* perceptions & presentations of information work. Chicago: Association of College & Research Libraries.

Leedy, P. D., & Ormrod, J. E. (2005). *Practical research: Planning and design* (8th ed.). Upper Saddle River, NJ: Pearson.

Lowe-Wincentsen, D. (2011). A finger in the pie: A look at how multiple careers benefit the library professional. In Martin K. Wallace, Rebecca Tolley-Stokes, & Erik Sean Estep (Eds.), *The Generation X librarian: Essays on leadership, technology, pop culture, social responsibility, and professional identity* (pp. 99–108). Jefferson, North Carolina: McFarland & Company.

Lynn, S. (2001). *Texts and contexts: Writing about literature with critical theory* (3rd ed.). New York: Addison-Wesley Educational Publishers.

Majid, S., & Haider, A. (2008). Image problem even haunts hi-tech libraries: Stereotypes associated with library and information professionals in Singapore. *Aslib Proceedings: New Information Perspectives, 60*(3), 229–241. doi:10.1108/00012530810879105

McCoy, T. (2014, July 21). Thousands of women, accused of sorcery, tortured, and executed in Indian witch hunts. *The Washington Post.* Retrieved from http://www.washingtonpost.com/news/morning-mix/wp/2014/07/21/thousands-of-women-accused-of-sorcery-tortured-and-executed-in-indian-witch-hunts/

McHugh, N.A. (2007). *Feminist philosophies A-Z.* Edinburgh: Edinburgh University Press.

Mehrer, E. G. (2013, October 11). Librarian tattoo calendar challenges stereotypes. Retrieved from http://www.huffingtonpost.com/emily-grace-mehrer/librarian-tattoo_b_4086088.html

Mizra, R., & Seale, M. (2011). Watchers, punks and dashing heroes: Representations of male librarians in Generation X mass culture. In Martin K. Wallace, Rebecca Tolley-Stokes, & Erik Sean Estep (Eds.), *The Generation X librarian: Essays on leadership, technology, pop culture, social responsibility, and professional identity* (pp. 135–146). Jefferson, North Carolina: McFarland & Company.

Myers, D.G. (2005). *Exploring psychology* (6th ed.). New York: Worth Publishers.

Nanda, S., & Warms, R.L. (2009). *Culture counts: A concise introduction to cultural anthropology.* Belmont, CA: Wadsworth, Cengage Learning.

Nealson, J., & Giroux, S.S. (2003). *The theory toolbox: Critical concepts for the humanities, arts, & social sciences.* New York: Rowman & Littlefield Publishers.

Neyer, L. (2014). Perceptions of value: A story from one Pennsylvania community. *Pennsylvania Libraries: Research & Practice, 2*(2), 108–112. doi:10.5195/palrap.2014.83

Office for Human Research Protection, & U.S. Department of Health and Human Services. (2004, September 24). Human subject regulations decision charts. Retrieved from http://www.hhs.gov/ohrp/policy/checklists/decisioncharts.html

Padavic, I., & Reskin, B. (2002). *Women and men at work* (2nd ed.). Thousand Oaks, California: Pine Forge Press.

Pagowsky, N., & DeFrain, E. (2014, June 3). Ice ice baby: Are librarian stereotypes freezing us out of instruction? Retrieved from http://www.inthelibrarywiththeleadpipe.org/2014/ice-ice-baby-2/

Pagowsky, N., & Rigby, M. (2014). Contextualizing ourselves: The identity politics of the librarian stereotype. In Nicole Pagowsky & Miriam Rigby (Eds.), *The librarian stereotype: Deconstructing perceptions & presentations of information work*. Chicago: Association of College & Research Libraries.

Pappas, E. (2014). Between barbarism and civilization: Librarians, tattoos, and social images. In *The librarian stereotype: Deconstructing perceptions & presentations of information work*. Chicago: Association of College & Research Libraries.

Parker, R.D. (2011). *How to interpret literature: Critical theory for literary and cultural studies* (2nd ed.). New York: Oxford University Press.

Parry, V. (2010, April 18). Were the "mad" heroines of literature really sane? Retrieved from http://news.bbc.co.uk/go/pr/fr/-/2/hi/health/8622367.stm

Pho, A., & Masland, T. (2014). The revolution will not be stereotyped: Changing perceptions through diversity. In Nicole Pagowsky & Miriam Rigby (Eds.), *The librarian stereotype: Deconstructing perceptions & presentations of information work*. Chicago: Association of College & Research Libraries.

Polit, D. F., & Beck, C. T. (2008). *Nursing research: Generating and assessing evidence for nursing practice* (8th ed.). Philadelphia: Lippincott Williams & Wilkins.

Posner, B. (2002). Know-it-all librarians. In Wendi Arrant & Candace R. Benefiel (Eds.), *The image and role of the librarian* (pp. 111–130). Binghamton, New York: The Haworth Information Press.

Poulin, E. (2008). A whole new world of freaks and geeks: Libraries and librarians on YouTube. *LIBRES Library and Information Science Electronic Journal, 18*(2), 1–11.

Pressley, L., Dale, J., & Kellam, L. (2014). At the corner of personality and competencies: Exploring professional personas for librarians. In Nicole Pagowsky & Miriam Rigby (Eds.), *The librarian stereotype: Deconstructing perceptions & presentations of information work*. Chicago: Association of College & Research Libraries.

Pyykkonen, P., Hyona, J., & van Gompel, R. P. G. (2010). Activating gender stereotypes during online spoken language processing: Evidence from visual world eye tracking. *Experimental Psychology, 57*(2), 126–133. doi:10.1027/1618-3169/a000016

Radford, M. L., & Radford, G. P. (1997). Power, knowledge, and fear: Feminism, Foucault, and the stereotype of the female librarian. *The Library Quarterly, 67*(3), 250–266.

Radford, M. L., & Radford, G. P. (2003). Librarians and party girls: Cultural studies and the meaning of the librarian. *The Library Quarterly, 73*(1), 54–69.

Roberto, K. R. (2014). Afterword: Toward a new inclusion in library work. In Nicole Pagowsky & Miriam Rigby (Eds.), *The librarian stereotype: Deconstructing perceptions & presentations of information work*. Chicago: Association of College & Research Libraries.

Roemer, R.C. (2015, August 12). New grads, meet new metrics: Why early career librarians should care about altmetrics & research impact. Retrieved from http://tinyurl.com/pshzyj5

Rydell, R. J., McConnell, A. R., & Beilock, S. L. (2009). Multiple social identities and stereotype threat: Imbalance, accessibility, and working memory. *Journal of Personality and Social Psychology, 96*(5), 949–966. doi:10.1037/a0014846

Sandstrom, K.L., Martin, D.D., & Fine, G.A. (2010). *Symbols, selves, and social reality: A symbolic interactionist approach to social psychology and sociology* (3rd ed.). New York: Oxford University Press.

Scherer, C. R., Heider, J. D., Skowronski, J. J., & Edlund, J. E. (2012). Trait expectancies and stereotype expectancies affect person memory similarly in a jury context. *The Journal of Social Psychology, 152*(5), 613–622.

Scott, A.F. (1986, Spring). Women and libraries. *The Journal of Library History (1974-1987), 21*(2), 400-405.

Seale, M. (2008). Old maids, policemen, and social rejects: Mass media representations and public perceptions of librarians. *Electronic Journal of Academic and Special Librarianship, 9*(1). Retrieved from http://southernlibrarianship.icaap.org/content/v09n01/seale_m01.html

Selfie, n. (2014, December). *OED Online*. Oxford: Oxford University Press.

Shaw, S. M., & Lee, J. (2007). *Women's voices, feminist visions: Classic and contemporary readings* (3rd ed.). New York: McGraw-Hill Companies.

Shiflett, L. (2000, Summer). Sense-making and library history. *Journal of Education for Library and Information Science, 41*(3), 254-259.

Smiley, J. (1984). *Duplicate keys*. New York: Fawcett Columbine.

Squires, D. D. (2014). From sensuous to sexy: The librarian in post-censorship print pornography. In Nicole Pagowsky & Miriam Rigby (Eds.), *The librarian stereotype: Deconstructing perceptions & presentations of information work*. Chicago: Association of College & Research Libraries.

Story, L. (2007, January 15). Anywhere the eye can see, it's likely to see an ad. *The New York Times*. Retrieved from http://www.nytimes.com/2007/01/15/business/media/15everywhere.html?

Tan, A. (2015, August 4). ILookLikeAnEngineer hashtag breaks down stereotypes, highlights diversity in the tech industry. *ABC News*. Retrieved from http://abcnews.go.com/Technology/ilooklikeanengineer-hashtag-breaks-stereotypes-highlights-diversity-tech-industry/story?id=32877688

Tancheva, K. (2005). Recasting the debate: The sign of the library in popular culture. *Libraries & Culture, 40*(4), 530–546.

Tevis, R., & Tevis, B. (2005). *The image of librarians in cinema, 1917-1999*. Jefferson, North Carolina: McFarland & Company.

Text, v. (2014, December). *OED Online*. Oxford: Oxford University Press.

Tobias, J. (2003). Ad lib: The advertised librarian. *Information Outlook, 7*(2), 12–18.

U.S. Bureau of Labor Statistics. (2014, January 8). Librarians. Retrieved from http://www/bls.gov/ooh/education-training-and-library/librarians.htm

U.S.C. Marshall (2015). The five laws of librarianship according to Dr. S.R. Ranganathan. *Master of Library and Information Science Online.* Retrieved from http://librarysciencedegree.usc.edu/resources/infographics/dr-s-r-ranganathans-five-laws-of-library-science/

Wade, L., & Sharp, G. (2010). Skull face and the self-fulfilling stereotype. *Contexts*, *9*(4), 80–81. doi:10.152/ctx.2010.9.4.80

Weaver, S. (2010a). The "other" laughs back: Humor and resistance in anti-racist comedy. *Sociology*, *44*(1), 31–48. doi:10.1177/0038038509351624

Weaver, S. (2010b). The reverse discourse and resistance of Asian comedians in the West. *Comedy Studies*, *1*(2), 149–157. doi:10.1386/cost.1.2.149_1

West, J. (2011). Hackers vs. librarians: Some thoughts on the privilege of 2.0 thinking. In Martin K. Wallace, Rebecca Tolley-Stokes, & Erik Sean Estep (Eds.), *The Generation X librarian: Essays on leadership, technology, pop culture, social responsibility, and professional identity* (pp. 126–134). Jefferson, North Carolina: McFarland & Company.

Whiteman, H. (2015, June 12). Female scientists prove just how #distractinglysexy they are. *CNN.com.* Retrieved from http://www.cnn.com/2015/06/11/world/women-science-distractingly-sexy/index.html?sr=fb061215distractinglysexy140aStoryLink

Williamson, J. (2002). Jungian/Myers-Briggs personality types of librarians in films. In Wendi Arrant & Candace R. Benefiel (Eds.), *The image and role of the librarian* (pp. 47–60). Binghamton, New York: The Haworth Information Press.

Willis, J., & Todorov, A. (2008). First impressions: Making up your mind after a 100-Ms exposure to a face. In Saul Kassin, Steven Fein, & Hazel Rose Markus (Eds.), *Readings in social psychology: The art and science of research* (4th ed., pp. 49–49). New York: Houghton Mifflin Company.

Yontz, E. (2002). Librarians in children's literature, 1909-2000. In Wendi Arrant & Candace R. Benefiel (Eds.), *The image and role of the librarian* (pp. 85–96). Binghamton, New York: The Haworth Information Press.

Zickhur, K., Rainie, L., Purcell, K., & Duggan, M. (2013). *How Americans value public libraries in their communities* (p. Summary of findings). Washington, D.C.: Pew Research Center. Retrieved from http://libraries.pewinternet.org/2013/12/11/libraries-in-communities/

Appendix

Librarians and Stereotypes Survey

Librarians and Stereotypes Survey

This anonymous survey is part of independent research being conducted about librarians and stereotypes; the survey is being administered in order to determine why librarians present themselves to the public, both online and in person, the way they do. There are also questions to gauge librarian opinion about stereotypes and how the public sees the profession. The survey is available between August 19, 2014, 2014, and September 19, 2014.

Please read the information that follows before beginning the survey.

For the purposes of this study, a librarian is someone who "helps people find information and conduct research for personal and professional use. Their job duties may change based on the type of library they work in" but include helping library patrons find resources and conduct searches, teaching information literacy classes, organizing collections, planning programs, indexing materials, collection development, preparing library budgets, training library employees, and providing reference services (Bureau of Labor Statistics, U.S. Department of Labor, 2014). Thus a librarian may not have the title "librarian" or work in a traditional library setting.

Survey results may be used in publication; any short answer responses that are quoted will be attributed to "a survey respondent," and no responses that could possibly identify you will be quoted. Submission of the survey indicates your consent to allow your responses to be anonymously quoted in publication.

Confidentiality Statement: This survey is completely anonymous. No personally identifying information and no IP addresses will be collected. Also, you are not required or encouraged to share any personal information for the short answer responses. Should you contact the researcher at any time with questions about the research, the researcher will dispose of any written communication or telephone messages upon resolving the issue in order to maintain anonymity and confidentiality. You are encouraged but in no way required to share this survey with your peers.

Opt-out Statement: Completion of this survey is completely voluntary. You do not need to complete the survey to share it, and you do not need to share it if you complete it. Also, if you decide to participate, you are only required to answer questions acknowledging reading the confidentiality and opt-out statements and acknowledging your consent to participate; all other questions may be skipped. You may also choose to end the survey at any time without submitting the answers to your questions.

If you have any questions about this research, please feel free to contact the researcher, Christina Steffy. Her contact information is below.

Researcher contact information:
Christina Steffy
cjsteffy@gmail.com
610.780.8836
www.linkedin.com/in/cjsteffy

Thank you for participating.

I have read the confidentiality statement, opt-out statement, and the researcher contact information.*
◯ True

I understand that completing this survey signifies my consent to participate and my agreement to answer questions honestly.*
◯ True

Please choose your age range.
- 18-24
- 25-35
- 36-45
- 46-50
- over 50

Please select your gender.
- Male
- Female

What is your official job title?
Examples: "Librarian," "Archivist," "Library Manager," "Archivist," "Information Specialist," "Bibliographic Manager," etc.

How many years have you spent working as a professional librarian (either with the title "librarian" or as a librarian but with another title)?
- Less than 1 year
- 1-5 years
- 6-10 years
- 11-15 years
- 16-20 years
- more than 20 years

What type of library do you work for? Check all that apply.
- School Library
- Public Library
- Academic Library
- Special Library (i.e. corporate, health sciences, law, etc.)
- Other:

Do you have your own online presence that is available for the public to view? Check all that apply. If you utilize something that is not listed, please check "Other" and feel free to tell what it is.
"Your own" means it is not sponsored by and it is not on behalf of your job or your institution. "Public" means that your page is not private; there are no restrictions on who may view your page

- No.
- Yes, I have a public LinkedIn page.
- Yes, I have a public blog.
- Yes, I have a public Facebook.
- Yes, I have a public Twitter.
- Yes, I have a public Pinterest.
- Yes, I have a public Instagram.
- Other:

Does this public online presence identify you as a librarian (or as your job title if your title is not "librarian")?
- Not applicable.
- Yes.
- No.

Do you use your public online presence to share personal and professional information?
"Personal information" is information unrelated to your job/field or to the library and information science (LIS) field. "Professional" information is information related to your job/field and to the LIS field.

- Yes, I share both personal and professional information.
- No, I only share personal information.
- No, I only share professional information.
- Not applicable.

Do you consciously consider librarian stereotypes when choosing how to present yourself to the public, face to face? The responses target both at work and outside of work behavior.
Think about whether or not stereotypes have influenced your interactions with people (i.e. manner of speech, patron discipline, enforcement of fines and circulation rules) or mode of dressing.

	Yes	No
When choosing wardrobe and accessories for work	○	○
When choosing wardrobe and accessories for outside of work	○	○
When interacting with people at work	○	○
When interacting with people outside of work	○	○

Do you intentionally, in person and/or online, try to present yourself in a way that disproves any librarian stereotypes? Please use the space below to say "Yes" or "No" and to explain your answer. If you can cite specific stereotype examples, please do.

Do you intentionally, in person and/or online, try to present yourself in a way that invokes any librarian stereotypes? Please use the space below to say "Yes" or "No" and to explain your answer. If you can cite specific stereotype examples, please do.

Why do you choose to represent yourself to the public, in person and/or online, the way you do? Please use the space below to explain.

What do you hope your representation of yourself, in person and/or online, does for the image of librarianship? Please use the space below to explain.

What stereotypes, if any, do you think people currently associate with librarians/librarianship? Please explain.

Do you think the patrons you serve (or attempt to serve) have a generally positive or generally negative view of librarians/librarianship?
- I think they have a generally positive view.
- I think they have a generally negative view.
- I think their views are generally neutral.
- I'm not sure whether they have a generally positive or a generally negative view.

Do you think the public overall has a generally positive or a generally negative view of librarians/librarianship?
- I think it has a generally positive view.
- I think it has a generally negative view.
- I think its views are generally neutral.
- I'm not sure whether it has a generally positive or a generally negative view.

How do you think stereotypes impact public perceptions of librarians/librarianship? Please explain.

How do you think stereotypes impact a librarian's ability to do his or her job? Please explain.

How do you think stereotypes of libraries/librarianship influence our personalities once we become librarians? Please explain.

How do you think stereotypes impact people's desire to become a librarian? Please explain.

What do you think are the best ways librarians can combat negative stereotypes? Please explain.

What type of impact do you think positive and/or neutral stereotypes have on the profession?

Please use this space to provide any other comments you have about librarians/librarianship and stereotypes.

ABOUT THE AUTHOR

Christina J. Steffy is the manager of library support services at the Pennsylvania College of Health Sciences in Lancaster, PA. Prior to that, she spent four years as a solo librarian at the Joseph F. McCloskey School of Nursing at Schuylkill Health in Pottsville, PA. She has also assumed a variety of leadership roles in the Pennsylvania Library Association's College and Research Division. In addition to her library work, Christina does freelance writing, editing, and public relations. She holds a Master of Library and Information Science from Rutgers University as well as bachelor's degrees in communications and professional writing from Kutztown University of Pennsylvania. For more information about Christina, visit www.linkedin.com/in/cjsteffy.

Photo by David J. Reimer, Sr.